Hand-Book to Newstead Abbey. [With plates.]

Thomas Bailey

Hand-Book to Newstead Abbey. [With plates.]

Bailey, Thomas
British Library, Historical Print Editions
British Library
1855
103 p. ; 12°.

Hand-Book

TO

Newstead Abbey.

BY THOMAS BAILEY.

HAND-BOOK
TO
NEWSTEAD ABBEY.

BY THOMAS BAILEY.

ENTERED AT STATIONERS' HALL.

LONDON:
SIMPKIN, MARSHALL, AND CO.;
NOTTINGHAM: W. F. GIBSON.
1855.

HAND-BOOK

TO

NEWSTEAD ABBEY

WHATEVER there may be, of praise or blame, due to the bulk of mankind for their reverence for the memories of men distinguished, among their cotemporaries, for the possession of great talents, or high attainments—sometimes sneeringly termed "Hero-worship"—it is certain that it is a principle so intimately interwoven with our very nature, that violence must be done to the moral instincts or sympathies of mankind, before this powerful feeling can be eradicated from our bosoms. There may be many errors in the life of the individual to mourn over—much even to condemn; still, the fact that he, whilst living, exercised a mighty influence over the hearts and minds of his fellow-men, will continue to rivet the attention of posterity to his name, and draw, through successive generations, the feet of the intellectual pilgrim to his home, or his grave; even when death has for long closed all personal intercourse between him and the world. Such is the case with respect to GEORGE GORDON BYRON. And though there is much to admire in the natural and artificial beauties of Newstead—much to gratify taste, and awaken feeling, irrespective of its direct relation to the name of Byron—yet it is unquestionable, that to the association, in the minds of most visitors, with this name is the venerable mansion itself, with its magnificent halls and chambers, chiefly indebted for the presence of great numbers of those who, from almost all parts of the earth, make pilgrimages to this shrine of departed genius. Had

George Gordon Byron been only what too many of his progenitors were, the inheritor of a noble name, and a time-honoured inheritance, whatever himself, or the present gallant and liberal-minded possessor of Newstead might have done, by the expenditure of money, and the display of fine taste to embellish or adorn the ancient abbey of the Augustine friars, it would have utterly failed to draw forth those deep feelings of affection, of romance, and regard, with which it is now, and, for ages to come, will be contemplated by the ardent, the generous, and the enlightened. Pictures, statues, and costly furniture might have attracted the idle gaze of wondering thousands; but the hallowed and hallowing feeling, to men of superior minds, that, whilst threading those stately rooms, they are, as it were, breathing the air of genius, and feeding their lofty spirits with thoughts instinct with intellectual life and energy, which is now the charm of Newstead, would have been utterly wanting. Such, we know, are the feelings with which a numerous class of persons visit Newstead, and wander with delight among the glories and beauties of the Home (transitorily as it was occupied by him) of the highly-gifted, though wayward, George Gordon Byron.

But it is not only Newstead itself that renders this short excursion from Nottingham a source of so much pleasure and instruction to enlightened visitors; there are many objects on the route of the traveller, brief as it is, to afford gratification to an inquisitive mind, and kindle imagination by their connection with the great operations of nature, in ages long since past, or their identity with the deeds and performances of existing power and worth, or the memories of the renowned and illustrious deceased.

On getting clear of the Station Yard—supposing the visitor to Newstead to be travelling by rail — the first object which attracts his attention will be the ancient castle of Nottingham,* and the bold and picturesque pile of rocks on which it stands. The Castle, though now in ruins, (having been burned by a lawless mob, in 1832, about the period of the passing of the Reform Bill,) is comparatively speaking, a modern erection, dating back no longer than 1679. It had, however, predecessors occupying

*Guide to Nottingham Castle, price 1s., published by W. F. Gibson, 25, Long row.

the same site, whose history is too full of striking and romantic incidents—of touching and spirit-stirring associations—of great and important events, national and local, to allow of being dwelt upon here. Suffice then to say, that from the period of the invasion of this country by the Duke of Normandy, down to the Revolution of 1688, when the Princess (afterwards Queen Anne) took up her residence within its walls, this spot was witness to the presence of more famous men—kings, warriors, and statesmen—and remarkable occurrences, than perhaps any other spot of ground in the kingdom, with the exception of London, and its immediate vicinity.

The lofty and precipitous rock on which the Castle is placed, as well as the long range of elevated ground, by which it is flanked, east and west, appears to have been the result of one of those mighty subsidences of the earth, at periods long antecedent to historic record, when the strong foundation of the rocks, in consequence of the existence of mighty caverns beneath, gave way, and the whole tract of ground, then as high as the adjacent surrounding hills, sunk to something like its present level, and the great valley of the Trent received its first formation, drawing into its bed the three great rivers, the Trent, the Soar, and the Derwent, which, before this event, in all probability, took a different course to the sea, to that they now pursue.

The next object of attention to the observant passenger will be the beautiful tract of ground lately known as the Park, but now about to be disposed of by its noble owner as sites for the erection of villa residences. At the north-west corner, the Cavalry Barracks will be seen; but, as on the expiration of the lease on which the site was granted to the nation, about 1792, it is understood their occupation will be discontinued, future travellers on this line may look for them in vain. The mysterious rock-holes in the foreground of the picture, with the pretty village of summer-houses and spots of pleasure-ground, locally known as the Fish-pond Gardens, will always form objects of pleasurable observation, or of curious speculation to the intelligent beholder.

The first commercial establishment we meet with on the route is the extensive bleaching premises of Messrs. Burton and Eames; a short distance from which are the works of Messrs. Manlove and Alliott, for the construction of hydro-extractors, and other machines. Proceeding about a mile, and immediately after entering on the curve by which we quit the direct Midland line from Nottingham to Rugby, we come in sight of a modern Gothic-built mansion called Lenton Priory, formerly the residence of William Stretton, Esq., a gentleman much distinguished, in his time, as an architect and an antiquary. Mr. Stretton possessed a fine taste in articles of *vertu*, and, at the time of his decease, was in possession of a large collection of rare and valuable works, in most departments of art, as well as a fine cabinet of geological and mineralogical specimens. Mr. Stretton's eldest son, Colonel Stretton (who has been dead a few years) distinguished himself much in the wars under the Duke of Wellington, and was aid-de-camp to his grace at the Battle of Waterloo. A younger brother of the gallant officer just named, and who has himself risen in the army to the rank of lieutenant-colonel, though now retired, has seen much service, and acquired much honour, in different parts of the world.

Lenton Priory is at this time occupied by Mr. Place, a commercial agent, whose place of business is in Nottingham. This mansion was at one period the dwelling of an extraordinary character, of the name of Roworth—at least, by such name he was generally known—though his true patronimic was *Watchorne.* He possessed a mild and engaging address; ready in conversation, and apt in pertinent remarks on men and things around him. To these favourable adjuncts to person was joined an easy and natural way of assuming different characters, and extraordinary facility in imitating various and opposite styles of hand-writing. These, at all times dangerous acquirements, he employed successfully for a while, as the means by which to maintain a genteel position in society; but eventually they brought him to ruin and an ignominious death. It was his practice, during the summer or autumn of each year, to leave home alone for about a month; on all other occasions taking his servant with him, and, frequently, the unfortunate female who presided over his household, and whom he dignified with the title of *wife.*

The alleged reason for this journey was to visit his tenantry, in some distant part of the country, and collect his rents: but the real object of it was, for the purpose of putting off forged bills of exchange, which he mostly contrived, as a commercial traveller, in the garb of a quaker, to get discounted at some of the provincial banks. By these means, in those days of easily acquired credit, he contrived, through several years, to live in the style of a gentleman, keep hunters, and indulge in expensive company. To cover the delusion at home, he carried on the business of a corn-factor, and regularly visited the markets of Nottingham, Derby, and Newark; in the vicinity of which latter place he resided for some time before coming to Lenton. But the details of the career of such a man as John Roworth, *alias* Watchorne, cannot be entered upon during this short excursion; especially as we have so much before us, and so little time to see and say all that will engage our attention in this interesting route. Suffice it then to state, that having in one of these *rent receiving* journeys perpetrated forgeries on two or three of the establishments of Attwood and Spooner, of Birmingham, as well as on two banks in Yorkshire, by which he netted from £1,000, to £1,200, the hue and cry was raised against him, and he was traced to Nottingham, and from thence to Lenton; but a friendly notice enabled him to quit home about five minutes before three or four policemen, and a couple of magistrates, were in possession of his house. Though the utmost vigilance was instantly employed to trace his whereabouts, he escaped detection for more than twelve months; and, like a second Eugene Aram, was at length found conducting a small school at a village in Yorkshire, still taking refuge under a broad brimmed hat, and a coat deficient in the canonical number of buttons, and the size of its collar. The identity not being sufficient to ensure conviction at Warwick, he was removed to York, where he was found guilty, and executed about the year 1817.

The village of Lenton, which we leave to the right hand, was, in the early periods of our history, distinguished for its noble Abbey, which, at the period of the Reformation, was the largest in the county, though scarcely a vestige of it is now in existence, founded for a society of Cluniac monks, by William Peverel, an illegitimate son of the Duke of Normandy, and governor of Nottingham Castle. Lenton, through the influence of the religious fraternity to whom it principally belonged, had many peculiar privileges conferred upon it, one of the most remarkable of which was, that during the period of its great fair, "no man might be allowed to buy or sell in Nottingham," on pain of severe penalties.

The new church at Lenton, with the parsonage, and commodious school-rooms, where nearly 400 boys and girls are regularly instructed in all the elementary branches of human learning, consistent with their sphere in society, and the principles of religion and virtue, under the careful superintendence of that excellent minister, the Rev. G. Browne, cannot fail to attract the notice of every passer-by, and awaken feelings of respect and gratitude to the excellent persons who raised these noble monuments of christian munificence, and consecrated them to the honour of God, and the benefit of their fellow-creatures.

Lenton contains several manufacturing establishments of a highly interesting character, besides those engaged in the staple trade of the district. Among these, near to the railway, may be particularly mentioned the Starch Works of Mr. Thomas Hall; those of Mr. Tucker, likewise engaged, on a large scale, in the same manufacture; and the leather mills of Messrs. Bayley and Shaw, whose improved method of dressing skins, and preparing them for the use of the bookbinder, the law-stationer, &c., is calculated to excite sentiments of wonder and delight at the contemplation of so much skill and ingenuity employed in the furtherance of so beneficial an object. Many of these skins, by a novel process, are each split into two or more sheets or skins, by which means an enormous reduction has been effected in the cost of vellum, for every purpose to which that material is applied. Another object worthy remarking, before we leave Lenton, is the excellent farming establishment of Mr. Wilkinson, and which abuts upon the line at the point where it crosses the turnpike-road from Nottingham to Derby. Mr. Wilkinson has long enjoyed the honourable reputation of being one of the most skilful practical agriculturists in the vicinity, and was some years ago famous for his breed of short-horned cattle; but being now considerably advanced in years, he has latterly declined the extensive prosecution of this part of his business, to which he was at one time so much devoted.

Having crossed the turnpike-road, before alluded to, we now enter on the parish of Radford, the united hamlets of which constitute the largest and most populous of the suburban villages by which Nottingham is surrounded. The population of Radford, according to the census of 1851, amounted to 12,637. This populous place, only sixty years ago, was a small rural village, occupied principally by colliers. The inhabitants are now almost exclusively engaged in manufactures, and some of the largest establishments connected with the Nottingham trade are within its limits. The great lace factory of the Messrs. Fisher employs nearly five hundred hands. The village is a real hive of industry, and is still rapidly on the increase, both as respects dwellings and population.

A short ride from Lenton brings us to the Radford Station, after which we pass the Radford branch of the Nottingham Gas Company's Works, the cotton-spinning establishment of William Wilson and Co., several extensive flour mills, and last of all "Grove House," seen through the trees at a short distance from the line, the residence of Mr. Sutton, proprietor of the *Nottingham Review* newspaper. "Grove House," with its tiny but pleasant lake and summer-house, (formerly, by some ill-natured or envious cynic, called "THE FOLLY") was erected, as a suburban retreat, by Mr. Elliott, of Nottingham, an eminent silk dyer and stocking-trimmer, who, from a very humble beginning, by superior skill and industry, amassed a very considerable fortune, which is now principally inherited by the Burnside family, of Gedling and Plumptre.

Parallel with "Grove House," on the rising ground above, is Radford Church, the grave-yard of which contains two or three peculiarly interesting monuments. The Rev. S. Creswell is vicar of the parish, which is a living of comparatively small value, and has no parsonage-house attached.

The traveller who takes an interest in the development of British commerce, and the maintenance and extension of that gigantic power, moral and material, which it is the glory of this country to possess among the great family of nations, founded principally upon the industrial skill of its inhabitants, aided by the immense resources of mineral wealth, with which it has been enriched by the hand of a bountiful Providence, will experience a sensation of no ordinary kind, as he learns that at this point he is first entering on the great coal-field of England. Seated in the carriage, and facing the engine, all the country, to the right hand and back of the passenger, so far as relates to coal, and nearly so as respects iron, (with the exception of the two small coal-fields of Leicestershire,) is a desert; whilst on the left hand, almost every acre, through immense tracts of land, abounds with one or both these important minerals—productions which, in a national point of view, are really worth more than the whole of the gold-fields and mines of precious metals and diamonds in the world put together, and multiplied ten-fold. What a magnificent thought is this respecting our once poor country! and how overwhelming the associations which crowd upon the mind of every reflecting person, whilst thus entering upon the great coal-field of England. The first works in this vast depository of national power and wealth, existing on this line, may be seen in operation near to Radford Station; they are of a very primitive description, and in all respects vastly inferior to those of which we shall shortly have to speak.

How wonderful is the extent of the beds of coal and ironstone, throughout the north and north-west of England, contemplated from this spot, compared with what is known to exist in any other region of the world! And then what strange and beautiful forms vegetable life appeared to manifest itself under, and how gigantic its size, at those remote periods of the world's history when the coal-measures were formed, in comparison with the existing species of the same genus of plants! proving incontestibly that, at such time, Britain, in its climate, must have enjoyed the vegetative power of a tropical sun. The study of the floral treasures of the coal deposits, from the perfect state in which they can frequently be obtained, even at a depth of many hundred feet below the surface of the earth, constitutes one of the most elegant and interesting sources of mental recreation to which a reflective mind can be devoted.

The coal formation commencing here, takes a course westward towards Belper and Alfreton, and onward to Chesterfield, Dronfield, Sheffield, Huddersfield, and Halifax, to Bradford. At some distance beyond this place it is lost, until it appears again beyond the valley of the Tees, where it extends across the Tyne, the Derwent, and the Wear, through Northumberland and Durham. The coal deposits of Lancashire form a considerable breadth, ranging east and west from Manchester, by Preston and Wigan, to near Liverpool, and are supposed to be connected at a great depth with the coal districts of Flintshire and Shrewsbury. The detached coal-fields of Ashby-de-la-Zouch, Coventry, Dudley, and Colebrook-Dale, the Clee Hills, the Forest of Dean, and King's Wood, are each, though in themselves comparatively of small extent, extremely valuable, several of them being highly productive. Almost the largest coal-field in Britain is the great oval tract of South Wales, from Pont-y-Pool to St. Bride's Bay, and which furnishes fuel to the stupendous iron-works of Merthyr, Tredegar, Neath, &c.

About a mile to the left hand, at the Radford Station, may be seen, through the trees, the grand palatial residence of Lord Middleton. This house, which was built by Sir Francis Willoughby, in 1588, is one of the noblest specimens of architectural grandeur in these kingdoms. Wollaton derives peculiar interest from the circumstance of it having been the birth-place and inheritance of Sir Hugh Willoughby, the first of the adventurous navigators of England who entered, in the last year of the reign of Edward VI., upon the perilous enterprise of exploring a route to China by the North Pole. The course pursued by Sir Hugh and his companion, Captain Chaloner, was, however, to sail eastward, instead of seeking, as has uniformly been the case, in more recent times, this *ignis-fatuus* of naval scientific enterprize, by steering westward. Sir Hugh, the commander of the expedition, with all his crew, lost their lives in the winter of 1554, at the harbour of Arzina, on the coast of Lapland, where they were frozen to death. Captain Chaloner, who was separated from his commander in a gale of wind, was driven through the Cattegat into the Baltic, and discovered the empire of Russia, or, as it was then called, Muscovy. It is said that Sir Hugh was found frozen to death, in a sitting posture, at his table, with all the ship's papers and his will before him, dated January, 1554.

Leaving Radford, and before arriving at the crossing over the Alfreton turnpike-road, the traveller will perceive, on his left hand, at about a quarter of a mile distant from the line, an ancient-looking mansion, nearly enveloped in the shade of a number of lofty trees; this is Aspley Hall, formerly the mansion of a branch of the Willoughby family, now the residence of Mr. Birkin, a merchant and manufacturer of Nottingham; a gentleman who, by the exercise of extraordinary skill and industry in the prosecution of his business, first as an operative lace-maker, and afterwards as a merchant-manufacturer, has been enabled, whilst yet comparatively a young man, to amass a very considerable fortune, and to be raised to the position of mayor of the borough of Nottingham.

Edward Willoughby, Esq., of Bloore Place, Kent, having married Winifred, the fourth daughter of Sir Francis Willoughby, of Wollaton, who died about the year 1672, the Aspley estate, with some other property, became the patrimony of the lady, and continued to be the inheritance, and the old hall the abode, of her descendants, down to about the year 1800; when, by the death of the venerable occupants, and the sunken fortunes of the family, the estate passed, by purchase, into the hands of Francis Lord Middleton, of Wollaton Hall. "His Honour" and "Madam Willoughby," for such were the distinctive titles of respect by which the couple were saluted by almost all classes of the community around them were, perhaps, the last persons in this neighbourhood who kept up that sort of open-house hospitality for the poor, on particular occasions, for which the mansions of our nobility and gentry had used anciently to be distinguished. Madam Willoughby was a woman of great spirit, of untiring industry, and, considering her limited means, and large family, of unbounded liberality; she was the almost sole manager of the farm, somewhat over three hundred acres, Mr. Willoughby himself taking little notice of agricultural affairs; she was likewise the nniversal adviser, doctress, and instructor of all the poor in her neighbourhood, never allowing her religion, though she and her husband were strict Roman Catholics, at all to interfere with her charities, or the exercise of her good offices. Previous to the time of the Roman Catholics being legally allowed the free exercise of their religion in public, Aspley Hall was the only place to which the small portion of the population in Nottingham, and its vicinity, who had the courage to maintain an open profession of communion with the proscribed faith, could assemble for worship with safety; and, accordingly, they had used to come, at stated periods, from all the villages round about, where any Roman Catholics resided, as likewise from the town itself, to this house, to celebrate Mass. As a priest was kept in the house, at the charge of "his honour Willoughby," and all the poor attendants at worship were uniformly invited to stay and dine at the Hall, considerable expense was unavoidably entailed upon the worthy occupants of the mansion. The great sacrifices thus made by Mr. Willoughby and his wife, in support of their religious principles, and for the purpose of affording an opportunity of attending worship to a body of persons who were almost universally poor, contributed, no doubt, to that embarrassment of their pecuniary affairs which, after their decease, was soon found to be the case. But it was not only to persons of their own religious community that "His Honour" and "Madam Willoughby," at particular seasons, opened their house, and supplied, without stint, the provisions of their liberal board. At Christmas, they gave away largely of the good things they possessed to the neighbouring poor, and scarcely ever sent away empty any who applied for cheer, from whatever distance the applicant might come. Shrovetide, however, was the true Carnival-time at Aspley Hall. Prayers over, and the morning meal despatched, the large fire-range of the kitchen, from end to end, was supplied with coal. Several vessels filled with pancake-batter, previously prepared, were brought forth from the pantry, panchions of lard placed on the dressers, and half-a-dozen frying-pans got ready for immediate use. Every poor woman of the villages of Cossall, Bilborough, and Trowel, who had not the means of providing pancakes at home, was made welcome, with all her children, however numerous, to Aspley Hall, to fry, and eat their fill. There was but one condition attached to the repast, that each mother should fry for her own family, and that in turning the cakes, no other means should be employed but tossing them, and catching the cakes again with the uncooked side downwards. This feat is seldom practised at the present day; but sixty or seventy years ago, it was frequently adopted by the fryers of pancakes. Seated in their high-backed chairs, on the vacant side of the kitchen, (which place "his honour and madam" uniformly occupied all the time the frying and eating were going on) the worthy couple enjoyed the fun of the many mishaps which occurred from the tossing of the pancakes, during the morning; and joined in the merry laughs which took place, as the cake sometimes fell upon the floor instead of into the pan, with as much glee as the most light-hearted of their visitors.

But alas! the joyous pancake-eatings of old Aspley Hall came to an end. Shrovetide returned; but no invitation to eat pancakes at the Hall ran from house to house through the adjacent villages. "His Honour" died; Madam Willoughby fell into difficulties, and at length died likewise; the family became dispersed; the doors closed; the fires extinct; the hearth cold; and the mansion itself became the home of a stranger! Hospitalities of this kind have come to be considered as the marks of a rude and half-civilized age; things which belonged to the past, but altogether unfitted for a period of refinement like that in which we live; still, they are things on which a few fond minds will yet delight to dwell, prolific as they are with tender and romantic associations of a bygone age, the habits and manners of which are never more to appear among us.

Passing the Alfreton Turnpike-road, and proceeding two or three hundred yards, the traveller, by casting his eyes to the left, will see on the rising ground, distant, it may be, about half a mile, embosomed amidst a cluster of majestic trees, an ancient mansion, now used as a farm-house. This is what remains of the once famous Broxtowe Hall—a place which gives the name to the "hundred," in which a large portion of the county, including the town of Nottingham, is situated. On this classic spot, a thousand years, and more, ago, our Anglo-Saxon forefathers (the freemen of the hundred) annually assembled, in deliberate council, to concert measures for the peace of the country, the preservation of life and property---to debate the amount of taxes to be granted to the sovereign---to register wills, and give instructions to the Wittenagemote, or national assembly of wise men, as to the course they were to pursue in matters of public concernment. It was this circumstance, in all probability, which caused the Wapentake in which it stands to be called after its name. How remarkable is the circumstance that this manor of Brocielstowe (now called Broxtowe) should have remained, as to population, in about the same state as it was ten or eleven centuries ago. Villages have swollen to the size of boroughs or cities; these again have run out with an inundation of houses that has flooded with an exuberant population the whole districts by which they were once surrounded; whilst Broxtowe remains about what it was, when our bold and far-seeing progenitors, of a bygone age, made it the place of their annual meetings. Broxtowe Hall, during the period of the civil wars, was erected into a small fort, occupied by the troops of the Parliament. The situation of this place, commanding as it does extensive views over all the adjacent country, was extremely important, as an outpost, to the larger fortress of Nottingham Castle; its possession, therefore, as we learn from Mrs. Hutchinson's *Memoirs*, was at all times watched with much care and jealousy.

Tradition tells a beautiful love-story, arising out of the occupation of Broxtowe by the Republican forces. The lover, who was likewise the commander of the fort, was a gallant and handsome young man, of gentle birth, though an uncompromising republican in politics, and a puritan in religious principle. The object of his affection was Agnes Willoughby, only daughter of the then recent occupier of Aspley Wood Hall, a Royalist and a Papist. Captain Thornhagh, son of the brave and virtuous officer, who acted so distinguished a part in many a bloody fray of that period, (and at length perished in battle with the Scots at Preston Pans,) had rescued the beautiful maiden from the rude hands of a party of wandering vagabonds—half soldiers and half robbers, who infested all parts of the country, during the time of the civil commotions—as she was returning to her home, after a visit of mercy, to the house of a poor sick man, at the adjacent village of Bilborough. Aroused by a cry of female distress, as he was walking, with his bible in his hand, at a short distance from the fort, in the cool of the evening, the gallant officer rushed forward towards the spot from whence the sounds proceeded, when he discovered a young female engaged in a struggle for her honour, if not for life, with two or three wretches, who had already hurled her to the ground. Drawing a pistol from his belt, he fired, and shot one of the ruffians, the other two making their escape over the fields, when the young officer, unwilling to leave his act of heroism and gallantry incomplete, undertook, on being informed of her name and parentage, to escort the terrified damsel to her father's house. Struck with her beauty, and impressed with the religious feeling that it was by an act of special overruling Providence that he was sent to her rescue, Captain Thornhagh, in spite of the difference of religious creed and political sentiment, which he was aware existed between himself and the inmates of Aspley Hall, could not dispossess his mind of the influence which the spell of her charms, and the extraordinary incidents which had thus brought them together, cast over it. Nor, had he alone felt the influence of that strange event which had thus exposed two youthful hearts to the thrill of emotions they had neither of them, at least in an equal degree, before experienced. The young Roundhead officer, in spite of his puritanical formality of dress, and, in some respects, of language and manners, was still handsome and accomplished: that he was brave and generous, too, he had given Agnes Willoughby sufficient proof, in that, without stopping to calculate personal risks, he had hazarded his own life, in order to save her from injury, if not from disgrace and death. Under such circumstances, could a woman's heart, at the impulse of the moment, do other than yield itself up to the tenderest of emotions? A call, by Captain Thornhagh, on a subsequent day, at Aspley, to inquire after the health of the rescued damsel, developed to him charms in her mind equal to those which were displayed in her person. Agnes saw, too, in her deliverer, even more of beauty and excellence of character, than she had before discovered. She could not but look upon him with more than admiration—with affection: yet the obtruding thought that he was a rebel and a heretic, compelled her painfully to check the rising passion within her heart. Religion in those days was an earnest thing; something that was believed, as well as professed—that was felt in the heart, as well as uttered by the lips; a thing for which men, aye, and tender women too, were content to suffer, and even to die. Nor was this profound feeling, this stern maintenance of a faith, believed by either party, though in direct opposition to each other, to be "that once delivered to the saints," less deeply seated in the heart of the Puritan, than in that of the Papist. It cannot, therefore, but be expected that the gallant Thornhagh, in his calmer moments, felt the same checks to the indulgence of the tender passion in favour of Agnes Willoughby, as the maiden experienced in reference to himself. Still they loved each other. Nor did the character of the young soldier, though viewed as a heretic, and the supporter of the usurpation, produce anything like the unfavourable impression upon the minds of the parents of the damsel as might, previously, have been expected. It is true, that though they honoured and respected him as the deliverer of their beloved child from the hands of lawless ruffians, and had never, seriously, even warned her against the impropriety of allowing the tender intimacy, which they could not but see was growing up between the young couple, from ripening into ardent affection; yet, in their solemn and solitary musings on the events passing before them, they never could bring their minds, at all, to tolerate the idea, of a "Roundhead" and a Puritan, a rebel, and a contemner of the venerable and holy faith themselves professed, and in which their daughter had been carefully educated, ever becoming that daughter's husband, and their son-in-law. Several stolen interviews between the lovers served but the more to influence the ardour of their passion for each other; and at the same time, as the period for decision drew nearer, to increase their embarrassment, by revealing to them the dangers and difficulties in which their union would involve them. They saw in each other all those natural and acquired excellencies of character, that

> "Fair high fancy forms, or lavish hearts can wish,
> Or looked they on the mind, or mind illumined face."

They, indeed, seemed made to love, and to be loved by each other; but love, the ordinary master passion of our nature, more especially in the heart of woman, was, in the solemn moments of deep reflection, met in each of their bosoms by a feeling stronger—when conscientiously cherished—than love itself, *the deep sense of religious duty;* the consideration of what was really owing to their faith, their profession, their God. Could Agnes Willoughby think of becoming a heretical Protestant—of abandoning the creed of her fathers, and her own deeply cherished faith; could she think of bringing up her children in ways which she now believed would lead them to eternal perdition; could she sacrifice all peace of mind on these important subjects—all religious consolation on earth, all hope of heaven in future, for a lover and husband; however much she admired, and loved, and honoured him as a man, a friend, and an earthly deliverer? She could not! The sacrifice might break her heart, but the cost might save her soul. Nor was the young officer, who had a great reputation among the troops, as a man, mighty in word and doctrine, and who regularly led his regiment in prayer, as well as in battle, a whit less straitened in mind than was the damsel. He sought the Lord often, with tears and deep anguish of spirit, for assistance and direction, in this, the most trying and critical of his whole life's affairs; but, as yet, he could find no comfort, nor direct answer to his prayers. He could not tear the image of the beautiful and accomplished maiden of Aspley Hall from his heart; and yet, he saw that his union with her all but an impossibility. It was on a morning, early in November, in the year 1645, that, after he had been seeking the Lord on his knees, for a considerable time, for direction on this important subject, he received an order from Colonel Hutchinson, the governor of Nottingham Castle, to join him with all possible speed, along with what ever number of men which could be spared from the fort at Broxtowe, preparatory to the attack

on the fortress of Shelford and Wiverton, on their way to the siege of Newark, then held in considerable force for the king. Captain Thornhagh had only just time, through the agency of the trusty person employed by him on all former occasions, in his communication with Agnes Willoughby, to inform the angel of his heart, of this new call of duty; to commend his love to her, and ask her prayers for his preservation; ere he was on his way to Nottingham Castle. Agnes received the message with a heavy heart. A deep foreboding of evil seemed to seize upon the maiden's spirit as she contemplated this dangerous enterprize. She retired to her chamber, and before the images of her patron saint, and that of the blessed virgin mother, she poured out the deep anguish of her overladen heart; mingled with fervent supplications for the preservation of her lover. The day following, the troops left Nottingham, *en route* for Newark; and, on the morning after, commenced making preparations for the assault on Shelford Manor-house; which had been converted into a fort, and, from its situation, was a place of considerable strength. In the storming of one of the half-moon batteries, erected by the besieged within the fort, and whilst performing prodigies of valour, at the head of his detachment, Captain Thornhagh received a musket ball in his breast, and, without uttering a word, fell never to rise again. The intelligence of the fall of the late commander of Broxtowe was not long in reaching that place; from whence the dismal tidings were speedily conveyed to Aspley Hall. Poor Agnes Willoughby received the information with a thrill of emotion which shook, to its very centre, her inmost soul; but her grief, outwardly, was expressed only by a flood of tears. But the man she loved and honoured—almost revered—had died by a sudden stroke, in battle, without time for repentance—a heretic; had died in open rebellion against his sovereign and his God! These were the solemn considerations which now sunk deep into her heart, and made her, at once, resolve to live a life of holy virginhood for his sake; and devote all her remaining days, to whatever extent her life might be prolonged, to prayer, and fasting, and almsgiving; if so be, that by the supplications of the saints in heaven, joined with her prayers, the mercy of God might rescue his precious soul from that utter perdition to which, she else feared, it would be inevitably doomed: and faithfully she kept her word. The maiden immediately flung aside all her dainty attire—clothed herself in sable habiliments of the lowliest possible construction, consistent with her station in life, abandoned all the vain and idle amusements of the world, and lived, for sixty years afterwards, in the performance of all good works: a perfect pattern in manners, temper, and disposition, of every christian grace which could adorn the female character. And, at length, in a ripe old age, amidst the tears and regrets of all who knew her, sank into the grave with a quiet spirit, in the cheering hope of yet meeting, in heaven, him she had so long and faithfully loved on earth.

Proceeding onward along the valley of the Leen, which has its rise in the grounds about Newstead, the train soon comes in view of the Basford Station. It is a remarkable circumstance, as indicative of the vast improvement which has taken place in the agriculture of this country during the last seventy years, that a writer, about 1785, speaking of the state of the land, then called Basford Moor, lying between the crossing at Bobber's Mill and Basford Church, to which the train is now rapidly approaching, estimates that, in the course of time, should proper means be taken to restrain the waters within due limits, the land, hereabouts, might rise to the value of *ten pounds* per acre in fee simple; it is at this time, on an average, worth seven times that amount. Basford Church, dedicated to St. Leodigarius, a famous French saint, is one of the most ancient, if not the very oldest in this district; having been founded by Philip, son of Safred, one of the captains in the train of William Peverel, a son of the Duke of Normandy, the governor of Nottingham Castle, immediately after the conquest. At the period of the Reformation the rectory of the parish was given to James Hardwicke, of Hardwicke Grange, in the county of Derby; whose daughter and heiress, afterwards Countess of Shrewsbury, the wife of four husbands, from all of whom she derived immense fortunes, so as to constitute her the richest lady in the land, carried the impropriation into the family of Cavendish, with whom it remained until the year 1813, when, on the demise of the late Lord George Cavendish, all his possessions in this parish were sold among different freeholders. The Duke of Newcastle is lord of the manor of Basford, and owner of the estate, purchased at the sale of property above referred to, liable to the sustentation of the chancel of the church. In the grave-yard attached to this ancient edifice, lie the remains of the oldest man Nottinghamshire has yet produced. Henry Ward, who died in 1736, aged 108 years. It is remarkable, that though entitled to the freedom of the town of Nottingham on attaining 21 years of age, he deferred being sworn a burgess until in his 106th year, when he qualified in order to vote at the great contested election, 1734.

On a rising ground, about 400 or 500 yards from the Railway, and about a quarter of a mile from Basford Church, is the hamlet of New Basford, one of the principal seats of the Bobbin Lace-manufacture. New Basford was the scene of a very tragical event, during the period when *Luddism*—the name by which the crime of frame-breaking was locally known—was so rife in this neighbourhood, in, and about the year 1817; when two men, the one a Luddite, and the other an innocent person, were shot dead. In a field immediately contiguous to New Basford, on the north-west side, anciently stood the mansion of William Eland, constable of Nottingham Castle, at the period of the seizure of Roger Mortimer, Earl of March. At this sequestered house, as it then was, being surrounded, on all sides, by a woodland district, part of the royal Forest of Sherwood, there is reason to believe the private interviews between the young king and his adherents were held, previous to the plan for the seizure of Mortimer being put into execution. The spot of ground (part of the ancient manor of Algarthorpe) is still recognized in the surveys of the parish, and other documents as "Eland Hall Close."

The magnificent and extensive works just erected, by the Nottingham Gas and Coke Company, on a piece of ground opposite to the church, are objects well deserving observation: they having several features, in point of scientific and architectural arrangement, not hitherto adopted in erections of this kind hereabouts. The total estimated expense of these works is about £60,000.

On entering the Basford Station-yard, and passing its tastefully-constructed gatehouse, there will be seen through the trees which border the small stream which separates the grounds from the Station-yard a large old-fashioned brick house, only the south end and back of the building, however, being visible from this point—the front of the mansion facing the west. This is the early home of Philip James Bailey, the author of *Festus;* and here it was that, before he had reached his twentieth year, a large portion of that extraordinary poem was written. Few works, perhaps, ever published, in any age, have exercised so great an influence over the rising intellect of the community among whom they were diffused as has *Festus*. Much difference of opinion, it is true, has been expressed by public writers, on the merits of this work; but that it is extensively read, and is rapidly increasing in popularity in this country, cannot be doubted; whilst in the United States, and throughout the whole continent of North America, from Canada to the Isthmus of Panama, its success is unprecedented in the annals of literature. Not less, in all probability, than *twenty* editions of *Festus* have been published in the States, several of them being very large issues, and others splendidly illustrated with a number of fine engravings, from designs by American artists, the type and binding being of an equally expensive character. In this country five large editions have been sold; and arrangements, it is understood, are being made for the simultaneous issue of two editions—one designed to meet the increasing demand for the work among the youthful classes engaged in business and manufactures, and the other for a more select class, and who, hitherto, have been the principal purchasers of the work. Twenty-five editions of an imaginative work, of the metaphysical character of *Festus*, published before its author had reached his thirty-seventh year, and circulated in every region upon earth where the English language is read or spoken, is a testimony to the lofty genius and profound erudition displayed in the composition of this poem, which may challenge popularity with the productions of the highly-gifted poet of Newstead, or that of any other man of genius which this favoured land has ever produced. Bailey, as a poet, had no dawn before the public; being, in this respect, altogether distinguished from Byron, and most other poets. Like a tropical sun, *Festus* burst at once upon the literary horizon of the world, broad, glowing, and full of glory and power. And though his disk might, at first, be somewhat marred by spots, which weakened the splendour of his opening beam, his advancing progress has cleared them mostly away, and thus enabled his genius to shine upon the world of mind with a ray, which is equally admired for its purity, reverenced for its sublimity, and welcomed for its benign and genial influence. The following are the terms in which a writer in one of the United States reviews, *The New York Literary World*, sums up the opinions of his countrymen on the merits of *Festus*. "It would appear from these opinions, which from their intensity, variety, and number, (upwards of fifty) are to us very surprising signs of the times that Mr. Bailey has not so much improved on, as happily superseded the authors of the books of *Job* and *Ecclesiastes*, of the *Divine Comedy*, of *Paradise Lost and Regained*, of *Dr. Faustus*, of *Hamlet*, of *Faust*, of *Don Juan*, *The Course of Time*, *St. Leon*, *The Jolly Beggars*, and the *Lives of the Angels*. He is more sublime and simple than Job; more royally witty and wise, more to the point than Solomon; more picturesque, more intense, more pathetic than Dante; more Miltonic (we have no other word) than Milton; more dreadful, more sonorous than Marlowe; more worldly wise, clever, and *svelt* than Goethe; more passionate, more eloquent, more impudent than Byron; more orthodox, more edifying, more precocious than Pollock; more absorptive and inveterate than Godwin; and more hearty, more tender, more of manhood all compact than Burns; more gay than Moore; more versatile than Shakspeare" "I know of no poem in any language," says a writer at the time of its first publication, "that can be compared with *Festus* in copiousness and variety of imagery. The universe is as rife with symbols to this poet, as it is with facts to the common observer. His illustrations, somewhat bold and towering as the mountains, are, at others soft, subtile, and delicate as the mists that clothe their summits. But better than this, with a truth, force, and simplicity seldom paralleled, we have here disclosed the very inmost life of a sincere and energetic mind. Metaphysical and pscycological speculations are, so to speak, actualized and verified by the earnestness and passion of the writer. There are few books in which what is so profound in its essence is rendered so familiar in its exposition." And a recent writer, in a review of Mr. Bailey's poem, thus expresses himself: "Before the glorious song of *Festus* the production of every living poet must stand in the back-ground. Unfetterd by the rules of his predecessors, Bailey has poured forth his soul penetrating words 'big with mighty thoughts' in a manner of his own. The genius and power of Bailey are versatile in the extreme. He passes at once, and without the slightest effort, 'from grave to gay, from lively to severe.' His command of rhyme is unrivalled. He calls up the spirits of rythm from the 'vasty deep' of his own soul, and they rise obedient to his will. Now he chaunts his song in tone and gait solemn as those of a Pope or Blair —now light and flippant as a Butler or a Gray—and again with the lively airiness, or fine swinging musical cadence of a Tennyson. The lyrics which occur in *Festus* are the most exquisite things of the class we ever read. We know nothing to compare with them in beauty and pathos, with the exception of those of Burns." With these testimonials to the genius and surpassing talents evinced in the composition of *Festus*, we shall quit the home of Philip James Bailey, and pursue our route.

The mansion on the right hand, a little beyond the gate-house, is the residence of the Rev. H. R. Pitman, the highly esteemed vicar of the parish. There being no parsonage-house attached to the living, this residence, with its miniature park like grounds, the property of the Nottingham Gas Company, has been judiciously engaged by the clergyman for his occupation.

After quitting the Station Yard, we pass, in rapid succession, several of the large bleaching establishments for which this village is famous. The first of these, with its pretty virandered dwelling, facing the road, is that of Mr. John Fox; the second, that of Messrs. Burton and Eames; the third, that of Messrs. Cox and Cartledge; and the fourth, that of Mrs. Milnes (relict of the late Mr. T. B. Milnes). Proceeding onward, about a quarter of a mile, we pass the chemical works of Mr. John Ford. Most of the sulphuric acid employed at the Bleach-yards, in this vicinity, is prepared at these works; as well as an extensive business being carried on in the manufacture of superphosphate of lime, for the use of agriculturists.

Immediately contiguous to these premises may be noticed a Branch Railway, ascending by gentle gradients in a direction towards the West. This line is the property of Thomas North, Esq., and leads to his gigantic Coal and Brick Works at Cinder (or Sinter) Hill. The coal works here, and those at Babbington, to which they are united by another private Railroad, are considered as amongst the best conducted and extensive establishments of the kind, under the proprietorship of one individual in the kingdom. It is to the credit of Mr. North, to which testimony has been borne by several Inspectors of pits and mines, that whilst so many and such frightful accidents have occurred at other "workings," owing to imperfect ventilation, and causes, frequently preventible by a due application of capital to purposes connected with the preservation of the health and lives of the miners, no such catastrophe has, at any time, occurred at his works; notwithstanding their great extent, and the vast number of men and boys constantly engaged in carrying on under-ground operations. Mr. Woodhouse, of Overseal, in the county of Derby, has the management of the pits entirely under his direction: to his skill and judgment, therefore, aided by the liberality of the proprietor, the exemption of these mines from those frightful accidents which have so awfully disfigured many other establishments of the kind may, under Providence, be mainly attributed. Some idea of the extent of these works, and the magnitude of Mr. North's commercial engagements, may be inferred from the fact that there are fourteen permanent or fixed steam engines, and three large locomotives, and 250 trucks, continually employed in carrying on their operations. The extent of Railway formed and used, exclusively, for the carrying on the business of this vast concern, runs over twenty-four miles; and what, perhaps, will appear more extraordinary, is the fact that nearly one-half of this extent, or 11¾ miles is situated under ground: in some instances at nearly

600 feet below the surface of the earth; the remainder being lines of communication between different portions of the works, or places of deposit for coals, previous to further transit. The total number of men and boys employed in carrying forward Mr. North's multifarious undertakings amount, on an average, to about 1,650: and the coal beds actually in working, or, for the working of which preparations, in one stage or other, are at this time in course of procedure, run under nearly 7,500 acres of land.

The next object on the line which attracts our attention, is the Basford Union Workhouse. This commodious, and well-ordered establishment, has attached to it eight acres of land; the whole of which is cultivated by the inmates of the house. The Basford Union is one of the largest rural unions in the kingdom, comprising a population of nearly 70,000 souls, comprehended in forty-three parishes, and extending over 88,940 acres, having a gross rateable annual value of £155,208. As proof of the generally humane and considerate manner in which the affairs of this great union are managed, as respects relief to the poor, by the Board of Guardians, it may be mentioned, that whilst the total number of cases relieved by them in the half-year ending 29th September, 1853, amounted to 2,552, only 277 persons were relieved in the Workhouse; of whom 207 were women and children, the total number of men compelled to take refuge in the Workhouse being but 70: out of which number not more than *six* or *seven*, or one in ten thousand of the gross population of the Union,' were really able-bodied men—or such as were able to take care of themselves, if left at large.

Leaving the Union Workhouse, a few minutes bring us to the Bulwell Station. The rectory-house,—inhabited by the curate of the parish, the rector himself being non-resident—stands on a rising ground to the right of the Station; and, a little beyond it, on a still higher eminence, is seen the Church; a very neat edifice, newly erected at a cost of £3,000. The Rev. A. Padley, of Bulwell Hall, contributed £600 of this sum; and Mrs. Bolton, the mother of Mrs. Padley, £300, besides which she most munificently bestowed an organ upon the church, with other gifts valued at £400 more.

At this place we enter upon the great Magnesian Limestone formation, one of the prominent members of the carboniferous system, which extends from this place, forward to Mansfield, where it assumes the more chrystaline form of Dolomite, and constitutes one of the most enduring materials for building existing in this kingdom. The Bulwell stone is coarse and granular; and though used for common architectural purposes, when it is very durable, is incapable of being worked very fine, or of sustaining anything approaching to really high finish.

Bulwell may well be proud of having given birth to Dr. Samuel Wright, an eminent medical practitioner, who died during the year 1853, in the prime of his life, and the full career of his fame and usefulness, at Birmingham. Few men ever possessed greater talents than Dr. Wright, or a more happy way of employing those talents with advantage to himself, and without being burdensome to others, or awakening jealousy among competitors for similar honours. Nor were his talents solely confined within the range of his medical studies. A ready and copious elocution, a sparkling wit, a cutting sarcasm, with great store of erudition upon almost all subjects which engage the attention of the scholar and man of science, there was scarcely any topic he could not handle with ease and familiarity; so there was no walk of life open to genius and industry, in the which he would not have been able to distinguish himself above almost all competitors. Whilst a student at Edinburgh, Dr. Wright twice obtained the annual prize of the Harveian Society for a medical essay; in one of which his competitor was the most learned physiologist living in this country. He was also elected *senior* president of the Royal Medical Society, which as a student's society is considered as standing altogether unrivalled in the world. This appointment, so ardently aspired after by the most accomplished *alumini* of the University, may justly be considered as proof positive of the high reputation that Dr. Wright enjoyed among the most jealous and discriminating of judges—namely, his fellow students. In 1840, he took his degree of Doctor of Medicine. Before proceeding to the degree, it is necessary for the candidate to write a thesis on some subject connected with medical science. Dr. Wright selected the popular drug *mercury* for the subject of his dissertation. So important were his researches, that he obtained one of the gold medals of the University for his thesis. Among many other valuable testimonials which were borne to the extraordinary talents of Dr. Wright, may be mentioned that he was presented with a diploma of membership in the Imperial Society of Physicians at Vienna, one of the first medical societies on the Continent of Europe, and the corresponding membership of the Medical Society of Genoa. At the time of his death, Dr. Wright held the situation of senior physician to the Queen's Hospital, at Birmingham. As a professor, his merits here were proved to be of the highest order. His eloquence, his power of luminous statement, and his singularly extensive reading on subjects that interested him, combined to make him a most efficient and popular teacher. His premature decease, whilst thus in the full career of his usefulness and honour, was a loss to be deplored, alike by his profession, his country, and the world.

On the rising ground, beyond the village, on the left hand, may be seen Bulwell-Wood Hall, an antique and singularly constructed building, formerly the residence of a junior member of the Byron family; but now the property of the Duke of Portland.

The Cotton Thread Manufactory of Mr. Cartledge, at the extremity of the village, employs a great number of hands, and has for long been celebrated for the superiority of its products.

Leaving Bulwell, we pass the extensive establishments of Mr. Allcock; where bleaching, the manufacture of flour, and grinding of bones, are each carried on upon a scale of considerable magnitude.

A short mile from this spot brings us to the Hucknall Station. This lordship was an ancient possession of the Byron family; now, principally, the property of the Duke of Portland. The church of this village contains the mortal remains of the poet, Byron, as likewise those of his mother, and some other members of his family.

Passing on from the Hucknall Station, we have a view, to the right hand, of the village of Papplewick, once the seat of an extensive Cotton Manufactory, of which James

Robinson, Esq., was the proprietor: the deserted mills, and the once thronged cottages of the work-people, are still standing in all their loneliness, and for the most part hastening to decay. At these mills steam power was first applied to the process of spinning cotton. Papplewick is the property of Andrew Montague, Esq. The Hall, built in 1787, the seat of J. A. Case, Esq., is an elegant stone edifice, in a beautiful park. Near the Lodge is a remarkable hollow rock, known, traditionally, as Robin Hood's Stable.

Continuing our journey, a few minutes longer, we arrive at the retired and picturesque village of Lynby, with its lofty maypole—the interesting relic of past days of rural festivity—and its two ancient stone crosses—mementos of the piety of the holy brotherhood of Newstead, by whom, in all probability, they were erected. Here we leave the Railway carriages to pursue their onward course to Mansfield; and take the wild but pleasant path that leads to the Abbey. As it is some distance to walk, we will strive to beguile the time by discoursing on the past history of this famous place, which has now a world-wide celebrity, as well as of the famous family which, through many generations, made it the principal place of their abode, and whose lives and fortunes are so much blended with the proud records of our common country.

Newstead Abbey, it is supposed, was founded by Henry II., about the year 1179, shortly after the murder of Thomas á Becket, as a salvo to his conscience, as well as a satisfaction to the church, for his participation in that ruthless and daring deed. Thoroton, in reference to the foundation of the Priory of Newstead, says: "King Henry the Second gave to Lenton Priory fourscore acres of essarts (inclosures) of Curtenhale, in Northamptonshire, and the Mill of Baccliffe, in exchange for the land of Papplewick, which he gave to the Canons of Newstead, in Sherwood, *which he there founded.* The Monks were Black Canons, of the order of St. Augustine, and the house was dedicated to God and Saint Mary." A sculptured image of the Virgin and Child still stands in a conspicuous niche of the ruined chapel: this, as well as several other specimens of early English sculpture, may yet be seen about the ancient edifice, in a fine state of preservation. In addition to the town of Papplewick, the king bestowed upon his *New-stede*, or Place, long and large tracks of ground lying about the said Monastery, within the forest; and a field of arable land called Abbey field, lying between the town of Papplewick and the said Monastery, besides conferring upon the Canons many other valuable immunities and privileges. King John, as well as several subsequent sovereigns, confirmed and enlarged their territories and privileges; in addition to which they had several other good benefactors, among whom, principally, were the following —Robert Lord Lexington, who gave the towns of Routhorne and Scarcliffe, in Derbyshire; William Cossall, who gave his manor of Cossall, and the wood of Bulwell, with divers tenements in Nottingham and Egmanton; John Longvillers, who gave Tuxford Church; Robert and Henry Edenstowe, (brothers) who gave North Muskham Manor, excepting the stipend of the chaplains at Edenstowe; Elias Breton, who gave divers tenements, &c., &c. Henry VIII., by his letters patent, (May 18, thirty-second of his reign) granted this house, with the manor of Papplewick, and rectory of the same, and all the closes about the priory in the Forest, and all in Newstead, Papplewick, and Lynby, &c., to Sir John Byron, Knight, and his heirs. The Abbey, from that period, down to 1818—when it was alienated by the late Lord George Gordon Noel Byron—continued to be the patrimony of this noble family, of whom, in their genealogical descent, we shall now proceed, for awhile, to discourse about.

The first was Ralph de Burun, whom the Doomsday-book shows to have held numerous manors in Nottinghamshire and Derbyshire, besides several tenements in the borough of Nottingham itself; his son was Hugh de Burun, father of Hugh and Roger; Hugh became a monk at Lenton, and Roger enjoyed the barony. This Roger married Nicola, the daughter of Roclend de Verdun. Robert de Burun, sometimes styled Lord of Horistan, (a castle held by him in Derbyshire, and some ruins of which are still in existence,) was his son. He married Cecilia, the daughter and heir of ———— de Clayton, in the county of Lancaster, by whom he had Sir Richard, the father of Sir James Byron, of Cadeney, in the county of Lincoln, who married Alice, the relict of John Comyn, of Ulseby, and Sir Robert Byron, Lord of Clayton, in right of his mother, who by Maud his wife had Sir John de Biron, who about the twenty-fourth of Edward I., was governor of York, and likewise of Dover; he married Joan, the widow of Sir Robert Holland, Knight, by whom he had Sir John de Biron, Lord of Clayton, who married Alice, the cousin and heir of Robert Banastre, of Hindley, in the said county of Lancaster. By her he had Sir Richard de Byron, of Cadenay, Lord of Clayton; his son and heir was Sir James Byron, Knight, who by his wife had Sir John Byron, Knight, who died without issue, and Sir Richard Byron, Lord of Clayton; who to his second wife had Joan, the daughter of William de Colwick, and heir of her brother Thomas, which brought this family to have considerable interest again in this county; and caused them to make Colwick the principal place of their residence, which it continued to be for about two centuries, until sold, during the civil wars, by the then possessor, to Sir John Musters, Knight. Several monuments of the Byron family are still to be seen in Colwick church. Sir Richard Byron left a son and heir called John le Byron, Knight, of Clayton, who by Margery his wife, had Sir Nicholas Byron, Knight, who married Alice, the daughter of Sir John Boteler, of Beausey, in the county of Lancaster, by whom he had Sir John Byron, who died without issue, 1488. He was a devoted adherent of the house of Lancaster; and was knighted by Henry VII., almost as soon as he began his reign; in addition to which he was made Constable of Nottingham Castle, Steward and Warden of Sherwood Forest, and all the parks and woods appertaining to the crown within the county of Nottingham, with a salary of £40 per annum. He was succeeded by his brother, Sir Nicholas Byron, of Colwick. He married Jane, the daughter of John Bassy, of Rougham, Lincolnshire, by whom he had Sir John Byron, steward of Manchester and Rochdale, and lieutenant of the Forest of Sherwood, (he was called "*Little Sir John with the great beard*") and to whom the Priory of Newstead was granted, as before said. His son and heir was Sir John Byron, of Newstead, who married Alice, the daughter of Nicholas Strelley, of Strelley, in this neighbourhood; and by her had Sir John

Byron, of Newstead, knighted by Queen Elizabeth. He married Margaret, the daughter of William Fitz-William, Lord-Deputy of Ireland, and was succeeded by his son Sir John Byron, who had to wife Anne, the daughter of Sir Richard Molyneux, Knight and Baronet, of Sefton, in the county of Lancaster, who brought him eleven sons and one daughter. He was succeeded by his eldest son, Sir John Byron; all these brothers were valiant men, and risked their lives in the service of the King during the wars between Charles and his parliament. William, the fourth son, was drowned coming from Ireland. Robert, the fifth son, was a colonel of Foot, and saw much service. Sir Philip, the seventh son, after many singular feats of bravery, was killed at the head of his regiment, in the general assault made by the parliamentary forces upon the city of York. He never went out with his regiment without telling them, that "brave men never accomplish anything who did not set about their work with a determination to conquer or perish." Thomas, the eighth son, was a man of great courage and very good conduct. He commanded the Prince of Wales's regiment in the fight near Stafford, where he received a severe wound in the thigh, whereby he was necessitated to be carried off the field.

But to return for a few minutes to Sir John, created Lord Byron. The twenty-first, James I., he was returned as one of the knights of the shire for the county of Nottingham; as also at the first parliament called by King Charles I., at whose coronation he was made a Knight of the Bath. The third of Charles I., he was again chosen one of the knights for the county of Nottingham; and being one of the lords of the bedchamber to his majesty, and by him held in high esteem, for his great courage and fidelity, he was, in the year 1641, made Lieutenant of the Tower of London. From this situation, however, through the jealousy of the House of Commons, he was compelled to be displaced. Sir John had served in the war of the Netherlands, where he had entrusted to him, by the States, the care of their ordnance and ammunition. On the breaking out of the war between Charles and his parliament, he repaired with a good body of men, with arms and ammunition, to the Standard raised by the king at Nottingham. From Nottinghamshire he passed with some troops to support the authority of the king at Oxford. He afterwards commanded the body of reserve at Edge Hill, where six of his brothers, besides himself, were engaged; and the victory of the royalist forces at Roundway Down, was chiefly owing to the bravery of Sir John Byron; who, at the head of his regiment, charged Sir Arthur Hazlerig's cuirassiers, and after a sharp conflict, that impenetrable regiment, as it was heretofore considered, was routed and chased completely off the field. In 1642, (19th November) he was engaged in the fight at Newberry, where he did the king much service, as well as in several subsequent affairs. By patent, bearing date at Oxford, 26th of October, 1643, he was advanced to the dignity of a baron of this realm, by the title of Lord Byron, of Rochdale, in the county of Lancaster, with remainder to his brothers. He was afterwards made field - marshal general of all his majesty's forces in the counties of Worcester, Cheshire, and North Wales. He was besieged in Chester Castle by the parliamentary forces under Cromwell, which he held out to the utmost extremity, and then obtained the most honourable terms of surrender. After the fall of Caernarvon, which he also held for the king, seeing all chance of maintaining the royal authority at an end, he retired beyond sea. The king made him governor to the Duke of York, and being at Paris, whilst his majesty was under confinement, he undertook, in conjunction with a number of persons in Scotland, favourable to the royal cause, to make a diversion in England, as well as to raise the royal standard, once more, among his old friends in Cheshire and North Wales. This scheme failing, his lordship returned to Paris, where he died without issue, in the year 1652.

Richard, Lord Byron, his brother, succeeded him. He was governor of Appleley Castle, in the county of Westmoreland, as also of Newark, in the county of Nottingham, where he performed many notable feats of military skill and bravery, in defending that important fortress against all the power of the parliamentary armies, until the conclusion of the war. He died 1679, and left by his first lady, Elizabeth, daughter of George Rossell, Esq., of Radcliffe-on-Trent, in the county of Nottingham, a son, William, Lord Byron, who succeeded him. He married Elizabeth, daughter of John Viscount Chaworth, of the kingdom of Ireland, and dying in 1736, was succeeded by his son William, fifth Lord Byron. This is the individual who was known, locally, by the unenviable sobriquet of, "*the wicked Lord Byron.*" His lordship had the misfortune to kill in a duel, arising out of a dispute about game, and the game laws, in which his lordship took the humane and popular side of the question against his neighbour, Mr. Chaworth: and certainly was more sinned against, than sinning, in the affair, as Mr. Chaworth, it was clear, on the trial, made two thrusts at him, before his lordship returned the assault. Neither was his lordship the first to provoke the duel. Mr. Chaworth was throughout the aggressor; and no doubt, at the onset, thought to acquire an easy victory over his less skilful rival, being well known as an expert swordsman. His lordship, who appears to have been of a stern and unforgiving temper, having quarreled with his son and heir, about his marriage with his cousin, the daughter of Admiral the Hon. John Byron, did everything in his power to deteriorate the value of the property of the Abbey, and the estate thereto adjoining, until restrained by an injunction of the Court of Chancery. The object of his resentment, however, did not live to come into possession of the manors or estates of the family, dying whilst quite a young man, twenty-two years before his father, (1779). He left an only son, called after his name,(William) a promising youth, who was killed, when about twenty years of age, at the beginning of the late French war, in an affair at Corsica; thus leaving the old lord without issue male. He died 19th of May, 1798, aged 76 years; and was succeeded by George Gordon Byron, whose father was John Byron, Esq., eldest son of Admiral John Byron, and a captain in the army. He married first, Amelia D'Arcy, daughter and sole heiress of Robert, fourth Earl of Holderness and Baron Conyers, and by her had Augusta, married to John Leigh, Esq., son of General Charles Leigh; he married secondly, Catherine Gordon, (lineally descended from the Earl of Huntley and the princess Jane Stuart, daughter of James II., of Scotland)

and by her (who died Aug., 1811) had issue GEORGE GORDON, 6th lord, born 22nd Jan., 1788.

Having thus traced the pedigree of the Byrons, from the first historical record of them down to the period of the birth of the celebrated individual whose genius has cast a more resplendent glory over their name, and caused it to be more known throughout the world than all the civil dignities attained, and feats of arms accomplished by all his progenitors put together; and having now reached the precincts of the venerable pile, which the piety of past ages reared to the honour of God, and the blessed Virgin, but which a change of circumstances, joined with the progress of taste and refinement, has converted into a magnificent private residence, where liberality and taste vie with each other for pre-eminence; we have become well prepared for the indulgence of those exquisite associations of the mind with the glories of the past, which such scenes as these, contemplated under all their peculiarity of case and circumstance, are well calculated to excite in every reflective mind, alive to the many precious and romantic associations with which almost every foot of the grounds around us is crowded. Before, therefore, entering upon the examination of the spacious galleries and venerable halls of the Abbey, it may not be uninteresting to the visitor to make a perambulation of the gardens and pleasure grounds with which the house is surrounded; as well as to visit the banks of the noble lake, which adds such a charm to the sylvan scenery of Newstead. Fringed with its woods, that bow their whispering heads to the soft cadence of the gentle waves that lave the flower-bestudded banks, and speckled over with wild aquatic birds, whose melancholy notes seem admirably in keeping with the general pensive character of the scene around, this broad sheet of water, with

> "Her great bright eye all silently
> Up to the fair sky cast,"

confers a charm upon the scenery of Newstead which can be equalled but in few other places. The lake is formed by obstructing the waters of a small rivulet, which descends from the upper grounds through the valley, and in all probability was, originally, the work of the old ecclesiastical inhabitants of the Abbey, where their own corn-mill was worked. A gently winding path commands a fine view of the lower lake, and leads to an aviary, in which are some splendid specimens of that beautiful plumaged bird, the pheasant. Leading from thence, the path brings us to one of those elegant and fanciful creations of modern rural taste, called a *Swiss Cottage.* Having left the cottage, and passed through the kitchen gardens, which, as well as everything else relating to this well-ordered and elegant establishment, are most judiciously laid out,and, generally, in remarkably good order, being plentifully supplied with water from several small fountains. Attention is next attracted by a melancholy-looking small sheet of water, which, with its surrounding shade of venerable sombre yews, probably as old as the Abbey itself, seems formed for the very purpose of chilling the glow of life down to the freezing-point of abstract gloomy solitude. This pool of water was, originally, no doubt the *stew,* or fish-pond of the ancient monks, where a stock was kept, readily and easily to be taken at any time, for the use of the table.

The dark grove of trees planted by the former noble occupant of the premises, who enjoys the unenviable distinction of being always designated as the "Wicked Lord," next claims our attention. In it are placed two leaden statues of Pan, and a female Satyr, which are really fine specimens of art; but, in bye-gone times, were understood, by the country people around, to be representations of the devil, set up in this solitary place to be worshipped by the much-dreaded individual before alluded to. But as the great attraction of Newstead, at the present day, lies in what relates to George Gordon Byron, the poet, and not to the "Wicked Lord," or any of his alleged mischievous conduct, we will not stop to dwell upon it, but pursue steadily the object of our visit, to learn everything we can respecting its late highly-gifted proprietor and occupant. Before we quit this grove, however, we must not fail to visit the tree, in the bark of which Lord Byron, during his last visit to the hall of his fathers, inscribed his own name and that of his beloved sister. The names "Byron," and "Augusta," may still be traced, though, by the growth of the tree, the bark, and, consequently, the letters are becoming so far expanded, as to render them much less distinct than was the case some years ago; and lest this precious relic of the noble poet—this sign manual of genius, written in one of its hours of industrious idleness, on a tablet of nature's own providing, should fall a victim to that love of carrying away a tangible memento of our travels, which so much pervades the minds of English men and women, Colonel Wildman has issued peremptory orders that no one shall be allowed to visit this spot without being accompanied by some person or other belonging to the establishment. What a proud testimony is this to the dignity of genius! What a noble tribute paid by the suffrage of the general members of the great family of man to their more intellectually endowed brethren—the men who, by the force of their own splendid talents alone, have been enabled to perform their own apotheosis, and with their living hand inscribe for themselves an imperishable name in the records of all future ages! Many a lofty, and many a tender name has been carved in the rind of some favourite tree, or on a spot of loved resort; but, surely, none was ever watched and guarded, or viewed with that reverence, as are the twelve letters which compose the names of *Byron* and *Augusta* on the tree at Newstead. Leaving now the "Mysterious Grove," with its "behoofed and behorned" wonder-exciting statues, and taking the road through another portion of the gardens, more picturesque and interesting than that before visited, we arrive within the enclosure which once formed the ancient chapel, and tread on holy ground. But how changed the scene! Instead of vaulted roof and "long drawn aisle"—the polished shaft and groined arch of the cunning workman—the sacred altar and the richly vested priesthood—we have the open canopy of heaven, stately trees, flowers, and ornamental shrubs, a grassy carpet, a company of chattering, laughing, pleasure-seeking visitors, and the tomb of a *favourite dog!* and, as we cannot but think every one jealous for the honour of Byron himself, must feel pleasure at contemplating *an empty vault*, which the poet had prepared as his own resting-place, beside his canine friend. The faithful animal whose bones rest in these once hallowed precincts, and whose life and character are communicated in beautiful language on a neat marble monument, was, when five years old, seized with a fit of madness, which, after a few days' duration, put an end to his life and services. His lordship thus announces the death of his dog to a friend:—"Boatswain is dead! he died in a state of madness, on the 18th, after suffering much, yet retaining all the gentleness of his nature to the last, never attempting to do the least injury to any one near him. I have now lost everything except old Murray."* By a will which his lordship executed in 1811, he directed that his own body should be buried in a vault which he had made for that purpose, near his faithful dog. The sale of the Abbey, it may be, put an end to this absurd and degrading purpose; though it can hardly be imagined that his survivors would have carried out his lordship's intentions, even had he died the possessor of Newstead. In 1813 he writes thus to a friend:—"I had built myself a bath and a *vault*, and now I shan't even be buried in it. It is odd we can't be certain of a *grave*, at least a particular one." The following is the inscription and epitaph upon the dog's monument:—

NEAR THIS SPOT
ARE DEPOSITED THE REMAINS OF ONE
WHO POSSESSED BEAUTY WITHOUT VANITY,
STRENGTH WITHOUT INSOLENCE,
COURAGE WITHOUT FEROCITY,
AND ALL THE VIRTUES OF MAN, WITHOUT HIS VICES.
THIS PRAISE, WHICH WOULD BE UNMEANING FLATTERY
IF INSCRIBED OVER HUMAN ASHES,
IS BUT A JUST TRIBUTE TO THE MEMORY OF
BOATSWAIN, A DOG,
WHO WAS BORN AT NEWFOUNDLAND, MAY 1803,
AND DIED AT NEWSTEAD ABBEY, NOV. 18, 1808.

When some proud son of man returns to earth,
Unknown to glory, but upheld by birth,
The sculptor's art exhausts the pomp of woe,
And storied urns record who rests below;

* A very old servant of the family, to whom his lordship was much attached. His kindness to Murray was remarkable. "I have more than once," says a gentleman, who was at the time a constant visitor at Newstead, "seen Lord Byron at the dinner table fill out a tumbler of Madeira, and hand it over his shoulder to Joe Murray, who stood behind his chair, saying, with a cordiality that brightened his whole countenance, "Here, my old fellow."

When all is done, upon the tomb is seen,
Not what he was, but what he should have been;
But the poor dog, in life the firmest friend,
The first to welcome, foremost to defend,
Whose honest heart is still his master's own,
Who labours, fights, lives, breathes for him alone,
Dishonoured falls, unnoticed all his worth,
Denied in heaven the soul he held on earth;
While man, vain insect! hopes to be forgiven,
And claims himself a sole exclusive heaven.
Oh, Man! thou feeble tenant of an hour,
Debased by slavery, or corrupt by power,
Who knows thee well must quit thee with disgust,
Degraded mass of animated dust!
Thy love is lust, thy friendship all a cheat,
Thy smiles hypocrisy, thy words deceit!
By nature vile, ennobled but by name,
Each kindred brute might bid thee blush for shame.
Ye! who perchance behold this simple urn,
Pass on—it honours none you wish to mourn:
To mark a friend's remains these stones arise;
I never knew but one,—and here he lies.

The next object of interest in the grounds is the "Byron Oak," a tree planted by the poet himself, on his first arrival at Newstead in 1798. His lordship ever after displayed a remarkable regard for this tree, influenced by the superstitious feeling to which, in spite of all his attainments and all his scepticism in matters of the highest moment, he could never entirely divest his mind, that as the tree flourished, or decayed, so should he; for to use his own words in reference to it on a particular occasion, "As it fares, so will my fortune." On re-visiting Newstead in 1807, he found his favourite plant sickly, dwindling, and almost choked up with weeds. He appeared much concerned at finding it in this sad plight, and poured forth his lamentations in these touching lines:

"Young oak, when I planted thee deep in the ground,
  I hoped that thy days would be longer than mine;
That thy dark waving branches would flourish around,
  And ivy thy trunk with its mantle entwine.

Such, such was my hope, when in infancy's years,
  On the land of my father's I rear'd thee with pride;
They are past, and I water thy stem with my tears,
  Thy decay, not the weeds that surround thee, can hide.

Shortly after Colonel Wildman took possession of Newstead, he noticed this tree, and thinking it rather out of place, said to a servant who was with him, "Here is a fine young oak, but it must be cut down, as it grows in an improper place." "I hope not, sir," said the man, "for it is one that my lord was so fond of, because he planted it himself." No doubt, but in the lapse of years, that this oak will become as celebrated, and fragments of it sought after with the same avidity as were cuttings of Pope's Willow, or Shakspere's Mulberry.

Having now viewed everything particularly worthy of notice in the gardens and grounds, as immediately connected with the remembrance of the master-spirit, whose destiny is so deeply associated with them, we will now enter the building.

THE ENTRANCE HALL

Is approached by a porch of elegant design, in what we may suppose to be the original style of architecture of the edifice. The room has a low groined ceiling, and contains a Canadian canoe, and two beautiful specimens of Egyptian granite, wrought in the form of pedestals.

THE MONKS PARLOUR—RECEPTION ROOM,

In which is deposited the visitors' book, containing an interesting collection of autographs of persons who, since the decease of Lord Byron, have visited the Abbey from all parts of the civilized world. On the wall of the principal staircase, is a large painting by J. R. Walker, late of Nottingham, of the meeting of Jacob and Rachael.

LORD BYRON'S BED ROOM

Is an object of interest to all visitors, more especially as it is said to be still kept in the same state as when occupied by his lordship. This room commands a fine view of the lake, with its accompanying scenery, and is well deserving the attention of visitors; of all the chambers in the house it was the one most likely to be chosen for a dormitory by a person of the cast of mind of Lord Byron. The walls are adorned with a portrait of Charles James Fox, and several views of Cambridge; but, in themselves of no great merit, as works of art. In the dressing-room adjoining, is a portrait of "Old Joe Murray," pipe in hand, which appears to be by Barber, and a spirited portrait of his lordship's friend, "Gentleman Jackson," the pugilist, under whom his lordship, with many other young noblemen and gentlemen of that day, took lessons in the art of boxing. In a letter to this "gentleman," written in 1808, the year he took possession of Newstead, his lordship says, "I should be very glad to see you here, but the house is filled with workmen, and undergoing a thorough repair."

THE HAUNTED CHAMBER

Is the next place generally shown to visitors. It is a dismal room, where, as it is commonly said by the guide, the spirit of a restless monk, (probably he whose skull the poet converted into a drinking-cup) still occasionally intrudes his ghostly presence; though none of the existing inmates of the establishment will vouch for ever having seen the renowned spectre. The bedstead, though not equal to some in the house, is deserving of notice, as a good specimen of English carving. In the room are portraits of Archbishops Chiceley, Arundel, and Pole, Queen Catherine Parr, and a few others. This, and the previously described chamber, were formerly the sleeping room and oratory of the Abbot of the Priory. We now enter

THE LIBRARY,

On one side of which hang four portraits by Sir Peter Lely, the Countess of Rutland, Eleanor Gwynne,—to whose influence over the second Charles, the country owes the noble establishment of Greenwich Hospital—Mrs. Hughes, the dramatist, and the Earl of Rutland. There is a portrait likewise of "Little Sir John Byron, with the long beard," the first lay proprietor of Newstead; as also two modern portraits, by Lonsdale—Colonel Wildman and George Wildman, Esq. Here is a curious bell, very massive, and probably of great antiquity, found in a Budhist Temple, at Ningpo, and presented to the colonel by his friend, Captain

Goldsmith, R.N. There is also a very unique specimen of the old English "Stirrup Cup," neatly mounted, and bearing a Latin inscription round it, with the date 1599. The three stained windows looking from the Library are objects worthy of the attention of the curious visitor, as they are a portion of the ancient Abbey windows. The marble mantel-piece in the same room, with its rich wreaths of grapes, is another object well deserving the notice of the *virtuoso;* as are likewise the antique chairs. There is also an elaborately-carved reading-desk, by Stevenson, of Mansfield, which, though falling short of the delicacy of touch prevailing in some of the carvings of this noble house, is, nevertheless, well entitled to the observation of the visitor. The books, though not extensive in number, nor, generally, either of a very rare or costly description, are mostly well selected. Quitting the Library, we pass into

THE EASTERN CORRIDOR,

Through a doorway surmounted by a noble specimen of carving, representing an elephant and warriors, with the standard of Austria. The figures are extremely spirited, and there is great breadth of action given to all their attitudes. An antique ebony couch, of curious workmanship, and several King Charles's chairs, of beautiful workmanship, surmounted by a crown royal, stand in the corridor; from which, by a few steps you ascend into

THE TAPESTRY BED ROOM,

In its present condition, a truly splendid apartment; stated to have been formed by the Byrons for the use of the second Charles, though there is not the smallest historical record to warrant the notion that his majesty was ever in this part of the country. Had it, however, been so, the then ruined fortunes of the Byrons—who were constantly money borrowers even before they left Colwick—would not have enabled them to make so expensive a demonstration of loyalty as the fitting up an apartment like this for the temporary use of their sovereign. The utter sweep-out of everything valuable in the house which had been made by William

Lord Byron, from whom, in all its ruin and desolation, Newstead descended to George Gordon Byron, utterly precludes the notion that anything approximating to the character of the furniture in this room, would have been allowed to remain. Be this as it may, however, there is a portrait of the swarthy monarch over the marble mantel-piece, and over the door is one of his royal mother, the self-willed beauty of France, to whose froward councils, and fatal influence, his father owed, perhaps, no small share of his misfortunes. The State Bed is surmounted by ostrich plumes, decorated with hangings and coverlet of the most costly and beautiful silk tapestry, all old French needle-work. The ceiling is richly decorated with the Byron arms; the centre of the various heraldic devices being a beautiful representation of the sky. The tapestry upon the walls is of the choicest and most beautiful description; two of the pieces being Bacchanalian subjects, and the other oriental. There is a splendid inlaid cabinet in this room; and from the window, which looks into the old cemetery of the Priory, a view of Boatswain's tomb is obtained.

THE TAPESTRY DRESSING-ROOM,

Adjoining, and communicating with the last-mentioned apartment, is hung with the most beautiful and artistically designed tapestry which is to be found throughout the whole of the suite of chambers. The work is divided into six compartments, representing different subjects. The figures, more especially that of TIME, in one of them, are delineated with great force and beauty, and well meriting every attention which can possibly be bestowed upon them during the period allowed for traversing the room. This apartment contains, also, a portrait of Sarah Jennings, the haughty and tyrannical Duchess of Marlborough, said to be by Sir Peter Lely. If this portrait really be from the pencil of Sir Peter, to whom ten times more portraits are ascribed than ever it had been possible for him to execute, it must have been done nearly a quarter of a century before she became Duchess of Marlborough, and of course when she was quite in her girlhood; as Sir Peter Lely died in 1680, and John Churchill, her husband, (the great Duke of Marlborough,) was not raised to the dukedom till 1702. In the lobby, adjoining this room, is an unfinished stained window, the work of the late lamented Lady Gardiner, and underneath is a rich ebony cabinet with marble slab. We next enter

KING EDWARD THE THIRD'S BED-ROOM.

This, which is a richly panelled room, is one of the most ancient in the Abbey; and, if tradition is to be depended upon, it remains in its principal features as it was at the period when that magnanimous prince used it as a dormitory in one of his visits to the forest of "merry Sherwood." It was, however, in all probability, Edward I. who occupied this room, rather than the third of that name. Of the later Edward being at the Abbey there is no certain proof; but that the first Edward was, there is an unquestionable fact, vouched for by the circumstance that a charter, granted to *John de Annesley*, bears date at Newstead, 4th October, in the eighth year of his reign. The mantel-piece consists of rich carved oak, surmounted by a large panel of carved heads of Saracens, each occupying a separate compartment, and all richly emblazoned in heraldic style. Here is a beautiful cabinet, inlaid with plate-glass mirrors, a dressing table covered with glass, and a tripod stand, all said to have been once the property of "good Queen Bess." The room contains several valuable portraits, including the following personages: Queen Mary, Mary Queen of Scots, Richard the Third, Henry the Fourth, Harry the Eighth, and the Duke D'Artois. The first two are charming little pictures, which perhaps we might venture to ascribe to Holbein; there being no artist of that time living in England besides Holbein who could execute works in the style of these portraits. As respects the portrait of the Duke D'Artois, there cannot be a doubt on the mind of any one, at all familiar with the history of painting, that the date (1338) is a gross anachronism.

THE BED-ROOM OF HIS ROYAL HIGHNESS THE LATE DUKE OF SUSSEX

Is distinguished, in the Abbey books, as "King Henry the Seventh's Lodgings," yet there is no historical evidence whatever to be adduced of that king ever having visited Newstead. He slept one night in the vicinity of Nottingham, prior to the battle of Stoke-field, but from the accounts transmitted to us, it is evident that it was at the house of one of his adherents, near to the town of Nottingham, where he held a council at the Castle, on the following day, in the midst of his troops, who were all gathered, or lodged, in the Meadows, south of the town, and the villages adjacent. Henry of Lancaster was too wary a soldier, and had too great a stake in the coming struggle, to leave his troops, in the midst of spies and enemies, to be at the trouble of riding a dozen or fourteen miles away from the line of his route, to pass his night in a dormitory, surrounded by a company of lazy monks, when he could have enjoyed the advantage of a more suitable lodging at the Abbey of Lenton, or the Castle of Nottingham, or the houses of some of his adherents south of the town. The room, however, is well deserving of notice, as possessing some very rich tapestry, representing Indian subjects; and an antique mantel-piece, of pannelled heads, similar to those in the best bed-room. There is, in addition, a handsome bedstead, with rich crimson drapery, the whole surmounted by a tasteful cornice, and plumes of ostrich feathers. A beautiful set of carved oak chairs, in the apartment, have seats worked by the hand of Mrs. Wildman, the accomplished lady of the mansion; and which, as a specimen of female labour, in the present day, is equally creditable to her taste and her industry. Over the door is a portrait of the unfortunate Duke of Monmouth; and in another part is a figure in a masquerade dress, *called* one of the Byron family; it may be safely affirmed that there never was a Byron but who was too proud to allow himself to be perpetuated to posterity in the dress of a mountebank, however, under peculiar circumstances, he might assume such a mask for the nonce.

THE DUKE OF SUSSEX'S SITTING-ROOM.

The consideration that in this apartment one of the most patriotic and enlightened members of the royal family of England, passed many hours of mental exercise in reading and study, must for long give it great interest in the mind of every true friend to his country. Another interesting feature of the room, though of a very inferior character to the last, is that it contains a fine portrait of the dog Boatswain. There is also a portrait of a soldier of the 7th Hussars, and his charger, several landscapes, and a sea-piece, all in good style of art, but making no pretensions to first-class pictures. Another beautiful cabinet, inlaid with ebony and tortoise-shell, adorns this room; as likewise a curious old oak chest. We now approach

THE GRAND DRAWING-ROOM.

So far as furniture and decoration, grandeur of construction, and splendour of embellishment go to make *Newstead Abbey* a place of fashionable resort to visitors from distant places, this room is by far the finest object of attraction in the house. The richly decorated and slightly coved ceiling, with massive oak framework springing boldly from corbels beautifully carved, the splendidly embossed compartments, and elegant pendants, combined with the glittering effect of a large lantern-shaped gilt chandelier, suspended in the centre, an assemblage of costly furniture, and richly framed paintings, heightened, in splendour of effect, by the smooth and highly polished oak floor, so bright that you may fear to set foot upon it, present a scene to the eye, and a stimulus to the imagination, which are hardly paralleled among the most celebrated seats of wealth and magnificence in this country. There are many as fine, and as magnificently furnished rooms as this to be found among the halls and mansions of the gentry and nobility of Britain; but there are few where, in addition to these captivating objects, there are so many deep and touching associations connected therewith, as crowd upon the mind whilst we are pacing this noble room, and the one into which we are next introduced. The east end of the Drawing-room is adorned with the following paintings: Dogs and Stag, a fine picture by *Oudsy*, Portrait of Thomas Wildman, Esq., M.P., (father of Colonel Wildman) by that very clever artist *Romney*, who lost his senses about a woman; the late Lady Hamilton—who was little better, to all those who were captivated by her charms, than a spirit of evil in the form of an angel of light. There is likewise a portrait of Lord

Heniker, by the same gifted artist; as also portraits of Lord and Lady Gardiner. Along the north side are portraits of George the First, Princess Dowager of Wales, (mother of George the Third) George the Second, Queen Mary, (wife of William the Third), the celebrated portrait of Lord Byron, the poet, by *Phillips;* William the Third, and George the Third, by *Ramsey;* and a fine portrait of the Earl of Arundel and Boy, by *Vandyke.* At the west end, as a centre-piece, is a full-length portrait of his late royal highness the Duke of Sussex, by *Lonsdale,* in massive gilt frame. This is a very noble work. The figure is remarkably well poised,—its attidude being firm, yet perfectly easy, the head well placed, the hands neatly drawn and finished, with a fine breadth of light diffused over it, which brings out its prominent parts in fine relief, while the chiarooscuro is chastely and naturally preserved. On either side are portraits of Sir Hildebrand Oaks, by *Russell,* and Colonel Edward Wildman, by the same artist; Colonel Wildman, by *Phillips,* and Mrs. Wildman, by *Lonsdale.* This is a splendid group of portraits, all true English characters, and all painted in that noble style of art for which first-class English portrait painters are distinguished beyond those of the continent of Europe. Between the windows, on the south side, is a picture of two young females with a child, said to be by *Vandyke.* Beneath the *Oudsy* painting, stands a gilt cabinet, richly inlaid with tortoise-shell and silver, now a depository for the far-famed cup, made by order of Lord Byron, during his residence at Newstead, out of the skull of a deceased monk, whose skeleton was found enclosed in a stone coffin. It is mounted in silver, and has engraved upon it the following inscription:

Start not, nor deem my spirit fled!
  In me behold the only skull
From which, unlike a living head,
  Whatever flows is never dull.

I lived, I loved, I quaffed like thee:
  I died: let earth my bones resign:
Fill up—thou can'st not injure me,
  The worm hath fouler lips than thine.

Better to hold the sparkling grape,
  Than nurse the earth-worm's slimy brood;
And circle in the goblet's shape
  The drink of gods, than reptile's food.

Where once my wit perchance hath shone,
  In aid of others let me shine;
And when, alas! our brains are gone,
  What nobler substitute than wine?

Quaff while thou can'st; another race,
  When thou and thine, like me art sped,
May rescue thee from earth's embrace,
  And rhyme and revel with the dead.

Why, no—since through life's little day,
  Our heads such sad effects produce!
Redeemed from worms and wasting clay,
  This chance is their's to be of use.

The chimney-piece of this room is a fine piece of sculpture, the subject being the story of Androcles and the Lion, with two finely wrought busts as jambs, or supporters, the whole being of exquisite Italian marble. There is a splendid gilt cabinet placed under the portrait of the Duke of Sussex, and an ebony and tortoise one opposite the fire-place. These beautiful and curious cabinets constitute quite a feature in the furniture of the apartments of this splendid residence, and, as they deserve to be, are mostly objects of great admiration by visitors, more especially by ladies. Under a glass-case is a model of a monument to Leopold the First, of Germany. It is of mother-of-pearl and ebony, and is as exquisitely designed as it is beautifully executed. There is likewise an elegant epergne in Sevres china, richly mounted in gold, and adorned with some very artistic paintings, (including a view of Newstead) by Lady Gardiner, the whole designed as a centre-piece for the table, and having plates to match (not shown), with illustrations by the same lady, recording the principal military events in the career of Colonel Wildman. Leaving this magnificent apartment, we descend, by a few polished oak steps, into the corridor, from which you enter the

GRAND DINING HALL,

A room of noble proportions, being the ancient refectory of

the Abbey. The ceiling displays bold oak frame-work springing from shield corbels, richly decorated with armorial bearings; while the walls are ornamented with suits and pieces of ancient and modern armour, stags' antlers, buffalo horns, &c., the whole producing a very grand and imposing effect. At one end is a fine Gothic screen, in three compartments, above which is the music gallery. The door-way leading from the west corridor is of the same style, and a very beautiful specimen of carving. The room is panelled in oak to the height of ten feet, and measures about fifty-four feet by twenty-four, and about thirty in height.

THE BREAKFAST ROOM,

Formerly used as Lord Byron's dining room. The ceiling of this apartment is richly emblazoned in azure and gold, in square compartments, and is ornamented by another of those beautiful and curious mantel-pieces, made up of a number of carved heads, in fine relief. In this instance the heads appear to be those of four of the old monarchs of this kingdom—Henry the Eighth, with two of his wives, or concubines, and the armorial bearings of the Byrons in the centre. The chairs are covered with tapestry, illustrating many of the fables of Æsop. There are two pictures to which the attention of the visitor is particularly called; one, a portrait of Rembrandt, painted by himself; and the other, an infant Saviour, by John Van Eyck, said to be *the finest specimen of this master in England.* Descending the stair-case, we are introduced into

THE CLOISTERS.

These cloisters, in their construction, exactly resemble those of Westminster Abbey, only they are on a smaller scale, but possessing, if possible, a more venerable appearance. Here many of the ancient inhabitants of this once famous abbey lie interred. These cloisters lead into an ancient and extensive crypt, under the body of the church, but which, through several generations of more recent occupants of the place, have been used as cellars; here also was the singing room for the use of the choristers.

THE CHAPEL

Was formerly the chapter-house of the Abbey. It is a small sombre room, the ceiling of which is a very handsome specimen of the style of springing Gothic arches. In it are three painted glass windows, containing effigies of the twelve apostles. The chapel, as well as the cloisters, appear to have been used, at one time, as a cemetery for the deceased brethren of the priory. In the centre of the cloisters is placed the ancient stone fountain, which formerly stood in front of the Abbey. You are likewise here shown the stone coffin, (as before noticed) from which was taken the skull, formed by Byron, in an hour of wanton disregard to the sympathies of our common humanity, into a drinking-cup.

THE SERVANTS' HALL

Has a handsome groined ceiling, and is interesting, as having formerly been the Xenodochium, where the lame, the blind, the aged, the halt, and the destitute poor, of all classes and ages, assembled to receive the charitable relief doled out to them by the reverend brethren.

Having seen what Newstead is *now*, we will just turn to the pages of Laird, who compiled the section of the *Beauties of England and Wales* devoted to Nottinghamshire, and see what he says of it at his visit in 1812, about four years after it came into the possession of George Gordon Lord Byron, his lordship at that time making it his place of residence:

"The front of the Abbey," he says, "has a most noble and majestic appearance, being built in the form of the west end of a cathedral, adorned with rich carvings and lofty pinnacles. The castellated stables and offices are still to be seen, as the visitor enters a sombre deserted court-yard, in the midst of which is a curious erection of red sandstone, in the form of an antique cross. In front is the west end of the ancient church; also the venerable front of the mansion with its towers and battlements, and Gothic windows; and on the right, some additional buildings in the castellated style, originally intended, for domestic affairs offices, but never in a greater state of ruin than the older parts of the house, yet assimilating well with it, particularly as being overshadowed with the darkening foliage of some lofty elms.

Ascending some steps, a heavy grated door and porch, open into the GREAT HALL, (the present splendid drawing or dining-room of the Abbey) quite in the antique style; its only ornaments are two pictures of a wolf-dog, and another from Newfoundland, favourites with his lordship. The little Drawing Room contains a few family pictures, still interesting from their locality. In this apartment there is a very ancient carved wood chimney-piece, in which are introduced four of the old monarchs of this kingdom, Henry the Eighth, and two of his concubines, and the family arms of Byron in the centre. The Gallery over the cloisters is very antique; and from its windows we see the cloister court, with a basin in the centre, used as a "stew" for fish. The Great Dining Room is a most noble apartment, presenting a good idea of ancient manners, but now deserted and forlorn. In passing towards the habitable part of the house, it was impossible not to feel something like an awful regret in passing the chamber of the venerable Mrs. Byron, (the poet's mother), exactly in the state as when she breathed her last in it, only a few days before; her clothes, her ornaments, were displayed, as if she had just retired; alas! retired to return no more! Our aged Ciceroni, (Old Joe Murray), with great good will, expressed a desire to show his Lordship's Study, and with all the respectful familiarity of an old domestic, went into the apartment to request his lordship's permission, which was readily and politely granted. It was impossible to enter this sweet little apartment without noticing some of the unusual ornaments for such a place; but, as the house itself is literally a mansion for the dead—for the cemetery of the monks was in the cloisters—it may account for the noble owner's taste in decorating it with the relics of the dead, instead of the more tasteful ornaments of bow-pots, and flower-vases. The other ornaments are some good classic busts, book-cases, with a select collection, and a very curious antique crucifix. A small Drawing Room, next to this apartment, contains some good modern paintings. A portrait of his lordship, as a sailor-boy, with rocks, and a beach scenery; some good sea-pieces; an exquisite Madonna, east and west views of Newstead, dogs, horses, &c. We now come to a long range of deserted apartments. In one, called King Edward the Third's Room, on account of that monarch having slept there, is a very ancient chimney, which, together with the whole fitting-up of the venerable apartment, seems to be coeval with the royal visit, and excites a most pleasing enthusiasm in the mind. Next to this, is the Sounding-gallery, so called from a very remarkable echo which it possesses. An ancient Gothic Greenhouse, with an antique roof, now opens into the garden, which was once the burying-ground of the church, and in which a large circular vault has lately been dug, with a handsome pedestal of white marble, on one side of which tells the passing stranger that it contains the body of a Newfoundland dog. This garden also includes the dilapidated part of the church, and is altogether a very interesting spot."

Such was Newstead only little more than forty years ago. What a contrast to its present magnificent appearance! There is, then, little that can be said to be truly Byronic within the whole mansion—the bed-chamber of the poet, with the celebrated cup, may, perhaps, be considered as constituting nearly the whole; all the rest is the creation of the fine taste and ample wealth of the present gallant owner and occupier of the Abbey. That little, however, is invaluable; as it, with the few memorials out-doors, still give, as it were, to the spirit of Byron, "a local habitation and a name" among the glories of Newstead.

Thomas Wildman, Esq., colonel in the army, was born 20th August, 1787; married in 1816, Louisa, daughter of Freesig, of Appenzal, in Switzerland. Colonel Wildman entered the army in the 7th Hussars, in 1808, and during that and the following year, served with his regiment in Spain, and was in the memorable retreat to Corunna. He subsequently participated in all the actions and affairs in which his regiment was engaged in the Peninsula, in 1813 and 1814; and had the honour of being aid-de-camp to the Marquis of Anglesea, at the battle of Waterloo. Colonel Wildman is a magistrate, and deputy-lieutenant for Nottingham, and served as high-sheriff in 1821.

The first wife of the father of the poet, and whom he had married under a divorce from her husband, the Marquis of Caermarthen, having died in 1784, he, in the following year, married Miss Catherine Gordon, only child and heiress of George Gordon, Esq., of Gight. In addition to the estate of Gight, this lady possessed, in ready-money, bank-shares, &c., no inconsiderable property; and it was known to be solely with a view of relieving himself from his debts, that Mr. Byron paid his addresses to her. On the occasion of her marriage there appeared a ballad, by some Scotch rhymer, which, as it bears testimony to the wealth of the lady, and the rakery and extravagance of her husband, may be here worth extracting:

MISS GORDON, OF GIGHT.

O whare are ye gaen, bonny Miss Gordon?
O where are ye gaen, sae bonny an' brau?
Ye've married, ye've married wi Johnny Byron,
To squander the lands o' Gight awa'

This youth is a rake, frae England he's come;
The Scots dinna ken his extraction ava;
He keeps up his misses, his landlord he duns,
That's fast drawen the lands of Gight awa'.
O whare are ye gaen, &c.

The shootin' o' guns, an' rattlin' o' drums,
The bugle in woods, the pipes in the ha',
The beagles a howlin', the hounds a growlin';
These soundings will soon gar Gight gang awa'.
O whare are ye gaen, &c.

Soon after the marriage, which took place in England, Mr. Byron and his lady removed to their estate in Scotland; and it was not long before the prognostics of the ballad maker began to be realized. The extent of that chasm of debt, in which her fortune was to be swallowed up, now opened upon the eyes of the ill-fated heiress. The creditors of Mr. Byron lost no time in pressing their demands; and not only was the whole of the ready-money, bank-shares, fisheries, &c., sacrificed to satisfy them, but a large sum raised by mortgage on the estate for the same purpose. In the summer of 1786, Mrs. Byron and her husband left Scotland to proceed to France; and in the following year, the estate of Gight itself was sold, and the whole of the purchase-money, £27,850, applied to the further payment of his debts—with the exception of a small sum vested in trustees for the use of Mrs. Byron, who thus found herself, within the short space of two years, reduced from competence, to a pittance of £150 per annum. On the 22nd of January, 1788, Mrs. Byron gave birth, in Holles-street, London, to her first and only child, George Gordon Byron. From London Mrs. Byron proceeded with her infant to Scotland; and in the year 1790, took up her residence in Aberdeen, where, soon after, she was joined by Captain Byron. Their union, however, not being, by any means, a happy one, a separation soon took place. Some time after this, Captain Byron again passed two or three months in Aberdeen, before his last departure for France. On both occasions, his chief object appears to have been to abstract, if possible, more money from the unfortunate woman, whom he had beggared and discarded; and so far was he successful, that during his last visit, narrow as were her means, she furnished him with the money necessary for his journey to Valenciennes, where, in the following year, 1791, he died. Notwithstanding all this ill-usuage, such was Mrs. Byron's lingering attachment to her worthless husband, that, on the intelligence of his death being communicated to her, she burst into an agony of grief, amounting almost to distraction; and her shrieks were so loud as to be heard in the street.

It was in the summer of 1798, that George Gordon Byron, then in his eleventh year, left Scotland—on the demise of his great uncle, the eccentric, and misanthropic Lord Byron—in company with his mother and nurse, to take possession of the ancient patrimony of his ancestors. They had already arrived at the Newstead toll-bar, and saw the woods of the estate stretching out far before them, when Mrs. Byron, from the window of the post-chaise in which they were travelling, enquired of the woman at the toll-house, to whom that fine estate belonged? To which she replied, that "it was the property of the Byrons, and that the last owner had been dead only a few months." "And who is the next heir?" asked the proud and happy mother. "They say," answered the woman, "it is a little boy who lives at Aberdeen." "And this is he, bless him!" exclaimed the nurse, no longer able to restrain herself, and turning with delight to kiss the young lord, who was seated on her lap.

"Even under the most favorable circumstances," remarks Mr. Moore, in his biography of Byron, "such an early elevation to rank would be but too likely to have a dangerous influence on the character; and the guidance under which young Byron entered upon his new station was, of all others, the least likely to lead him safely through its perils and temptations. His mother, without judgment or self-command, alternately spoiled him by indulgence, and irritated—or what was worse—amused him by her violence."

When Mrs. Byron, who was a short and corpulent person, with an awkward rolling gait, would, in a rage, endeavour to catch him for the purpose of inflicting punishment, the young urchin, proud—notwithstanding his lameness—of being able to outstrip the lady, would run round the room laughing, and mocking all her menaces. One of the most striking passages relating to his mother, in the few pages of that memoir which he left behind him relating to his boyish days, is, where, in speaking of his own sensitiveness, on the subject of his deformed foot, he describes the horror and humiliation that came over him, when his mother, in one of her fits of passion, called him "a lame brat." On their arrival from Scotland, Mrs. Byron, with the hope of having his lameness removed, placed her son under the care of a person in Nottingham, who professed the cure of such cases. The name of this man was Lavender, a mere empirical pretender to the art of surgery; and who will be remembered by many of the Nottingham readers of this *Hand-book*, as residing in Parliament-street. That the boy might not, during this interval, lose ground in his education, he received instruction in Latin from Mr. Rogers, the well-known conductor, for many years, of a large and flourishing seminary in St. James's-street, Nottingham; Mrs. Byron and her son, at the time, having lodgings at the top of the street, near to the General Hospital. Whilst residing here, it was their frequent practice to walk in the Park, where the writer of this has seen Mrs. Byron, the young lord, and the nurse, several times together. At that period the boy walked very lame, and had a pale and pensive cast of features. As a *boy lord*, in the common dress of the merely respectable youths around him, was not an every-day sight to a school-boy in an humble position in life, he well recollects noticing him with peculiar interest, as likewise the lady, his mother, a somewhat untidy, shabbily-genteel dressed person, and even following them, or walking at a short space from the party, in order the more particularly to observe them. The much conversation that for long had been abroad respecting the doings and character of the deceased Lord Byron, will easily account for the curiosity awakened in the mind of an inquisitive youth, to look upon one, of similar age to himself, who bore such a distinguished name, and was the successor to the estates of Newstead. With Mr. Rogers, young Byron read parts of *Cicero* and *Virgil*, and he always represented his proficiency, as compared with that of other boys of his age, to be very satisfactory. It was about this period, according to his nurse, Mary Gray, that the first symptoms towards rhyming showed itself in the young lord; and the occasion which she stated, as having given rise to this childish effort, was as follows: An elderly lady, who was in the habit of visiting his mother, had several times made use of expressions which very much affronted him; and these slights he generally resented violently and implacably. The old lady had some curious notions respecting the future state of existence, believing that the soul, on its departure from the body, proceeded direct to the moon, where it awaited its final destination. One day, after the repetition of those reproofs to the boy, which he construed into insults, he appeared before his nurse in a violent rage. "Well, my little hero," she asked, "what is the matter with you now?" Upon which he answered, "This old woman had put him in a terrible passion, that he could not bear the sight of her," &c., &c. And then broke out into the following doggerel, which he repeated over and over, as if delighted with the new vent he had found for his wrath:

> "In Nottingham county there lives on Swine's Green,
> As curst an old lady* as ever was seen;
> And when she does die, which I hope will be soon,
> She firmly believes she will go to the moon."

Finding but little benefit, though the boy had undergone a great deal of punishment, from the Nottingham practitioner, Mrs. Byron, in the summer of the year 1799, thought it right to remove her son to London, where, at the suggestion of Lord Carlisle, one of his trustees, or guardians, he was put under the care of Dr. Baillie; he was, at the same time, for the improvement of his education, placed under the tuition of Dr. Glennie, at Dulwich. Here the foolish fondness of his mother, and her continued endeavours to keep him from school, created a serious obstacle to the steady prosecution of his studies.

It was probably during one of the vacations of this year, that the boyish love for his young cousin, Miss Parker, to

*The old lady here alluded to, was the Honourable Mrs. Byron, aunt to the young lord's father, and who lived with her two daughters, at a house at the top of Pelham-street, Nottingham, adjoining to the open space, now forming part of Carlton-street, then known by the name of *Swine's Green*.

which he attributes the glory of having first inspired him with poetry, took possession of his fancy. "My first dash into poetry," he says, "was as early as 1800. It was the ebullition of a passion for my first cousin, Margaret Parker, one of the most beautiful of evanescent beings. I have long forgotten the verses, but it would be difficult for me to forget her dark eyes, her long eye-lashes, her completely Greek cast of face and figure! I was then about twelve, she rather older, perhaps a year." He had been nearly two years under the tuition of Dr. Glennie, when his mother, discontented at the slowness of his progress—though being herself the principal cause of it—entreated the Earl of Carlisle to have him removed to a public school. Accordingly, he was sent to Harrow. About the time when young Byron was removed for his education to London, his nurse, Mary Gray, left the service of Mrs. Byron, and returned to Scotland. As a mark of gratitude for her attention to him, Byron had, in parting with Mary Gray, presented her with his watch—the first he had ever possessed. The affectionate boy also presented her with a full length miniature of himself, painted by an artist of Edinburgh, in 1795, and which represents him standing with a bow and arrows in his hand, and a profusion of hair falling over his shoulders. To a shy disposition, such as was Byron's, in his youth—and such as, to a certain degree, it continued through all his life—the transition from a quiet establishment like that of Dulwich Grove, to the bustle of a great public school, was sufficiently trying. Accordingly, we find from his own account, that, for the first year-and-a-half he "hated Harrow." The activity, however, and sociableness of his nature, soon conquered this repugnance; and from being, as he himself says, "a most unpopular boy," he rose at length to be the leader in all the sports, schemes, and mischief of the school.

Having now arrived at a highly interesting epoch in the life of the youthful Byron, a short time may, perhaps, be not unpleasantly spent in running over a few of the notices of his school-life, which were collected by Moore, from various memoranda in note-books the poet left behind him.—"At school," he says, "I was remarked for the extent and readiness of my *general* information; but, in all other respects, idle;

capable of great sudden exertions, but of few continuous drudgeries. My qualities were much more oratorical and martial than poetical, and Dr. Drury, my grand patron, (our head master), had a great notion that I should turn out an orator, from my fluency, my turbulence, my voice, my copiousness of declamation, and my action. I remember that my first declamation astonished him into some unwonted and sudden compliments, before the declaimers at our first rehearsal. My first Harrow verses, (that is English as exercises), a translation of a chorus from the Prometheus of Æschylus, was received by him but coolly; no one had the least idea that I should subside into poesy."

"Peel, the orator and statesman, was my form-fellow, and we were both at the top of our remove. We were on good terms, but his brother was my intimate friend. There were always great hopes of Peel amongst us all, both masters and scholars, and he has not disappointed them. As a scholar, he was greatly my superior; as a declaimer and actor, I was reckoned at least his equal; as a schoolboy, *out* of school, I was always *in* scrapes, *he never;* and *in school* he *always knew his lessons*, and I rarely—but when I knew it, I knew it nearly as well. In general information, history, &c., &c., I think I was his superior, as well as of most boys of my standing."

The following extract is from another of his manuscript journals—"At Harrow I fought my way very fairly; I think I lost but one battle out of seven, and that was to H——, and the rascal did not win it but by the unfair treatment of his own boarding-house, where we boxed. I had not even a second. I never forgave him, and should be sorry to meet him now, as I am sure we should quarrel. My most memorable combats were with Morgan, Rice, Rainsford, and Lord Jocelyn, but we were always friendly afterwards."

"While Lord Byron," says Mr. Moore, "and Peel were at Harrow together, a tyrant, some years older, whose name was ******, claimed a right to *fag* little Peel, which claim Peel resisted. His resistance, however, was in vain; ****** not only subdued him, but determined also to punish the refractory slave, and proceeded forthwith to put his determination in practice, by inflicting a kind of bastinado on the inner fleshy side of the boy's arm, which, during the operation, was twisted round with some degree of technical skill, to render the pain more acute. While the stripes were succeeding each other, and poor Peel writhing under them, Byron saw and felt for his friend; and although he knew that he was not strong enough to fight the school despot, with any chance of success, and that it was dangerous even to approach him, he advanced to the scene of action, and with a blush of rage, tears in his eyes, and a voice trembling between terror and indignation, asked very humbly if ****** would be pleased to tell him 'how many stripes he meant to inflict.' 'Why,' returned the executioner, 'you little rascal, what is that to you?' 'Because, if you please,' said Byron, holding out his arm, 'I would take half.'"

Among those whom the youthful Byron attached to himself at Harrow, by acting the part of a protector, was a little boy, named William Harness, who, at the time of entering the school, was ten years of age, whilst Byron was fourteen. Young Harness, still lame from an accident of his childhood, and but just recovered from a severe illness, was ill fitted to struggle with the difficulties of a public school; and Byron, seeing him one day bullied by a boy much older and stronger than himself, interfered, and took his part. The next day, as the little fellow was standing alone, Byron came to him, and said, "Harness, if any one bullies you, tell me, and I'll thrash him if I can." The young champion kept his word, and they were from this time, notwithstanding the difference of their ages, inseparable friends.

"It was in the year 1803," says his biographer, "that the heart of Byron, already twice possessed with the childish notion that it loved, conceived an attachment which, young as he was even then for such a feeling, sunk so deep into his mind, as to give a colour to all his future life. That unsuccessful loves are generally the most lasting, is a truth, however sad, which did not require this instance to confirm. To the same cause, I fear, must be traced the perfect innocence and romance which distinguish this very early attachment to Miss Chaworth, from the many others that succeeded, without effacing it from his heart; making it the only one whose details can be entered into with safety, or whose results, however darkening to himself, can be dwelt upon with pleasurable interest by others."

On leaving Bath, Mrs Byron again took up her abode in lodgings, in Nottingham—Newstead Abbey being at that time let to Lord Grey de Ruthven, and during the Harrow vacations of this year, she was joined there by her son. So attached was he to Newstead, that even to be in its neighbourhood was a delight to him. An intimacy soon grew up between the young lord and his noble tenant, and an apartment in the Abbey was, henceforth, always at his command. To the family of Miss Chaworth, who resided at Annesley, in the immediate neighbourhood of Newstead, he had been made known some time before, in London, and now renewed his acquaintance with them. The young heiress herself combined, with the many worldly advantages that encircled her, much personal beauty, and a disposition the most amiable and attaching. Though already fully alive to her charms, it was at the period of which we are speaking, that the young poet, then in his sixteenth year, while the object of his admiration was about two years older, seems to have drunk deepest of that fascination whose effects were to be so lasting—six short summer weeks, which he now passed in her company, being sufficient to lay the foundation of a feeling that lasted through life. He used at first, though offered a bed at Annesley, to return every night to Newstead to sleep. At length, one evening, he said gravely to Miss Chaworth and her cousin, "In going home last night I saw a *bogie;*" which Scottish term being unintelligible to the young ladies, he explained that he had seen a *ghost,* and would not, therefore, return to Newstead that evening. From this time he always slept at Annesley, during the remainder of his visit, which was interrupted only by a short excursion to Matlock and Castleton, in which he had the happiness of accompanying Miss Chaworth and her party. His time at Annesley was mostly passed in riding with Miss Chaworth and her cousin, or in some trifling amusements or recreations in-doors. But his chief delight was in sitting to hear Miss Chaworth play; and the pretty Welsh air, "Mary Anne," was (partly, of course, on account of the name), his special favourite. During all this time he had the pain of knowing that the heart of her he loved was occupied by another—that as he himself expresses it,

"Her sighs were not for him; to her he was
Even as a brother—but no more."

If he at any time had flattered himself with the hope of being loved by her, a circumstance mentioned in his *memoranda*, as one of the most painful of those humiliations to which his foot exposed him, must have let in the truth with dreadful certainty upon his heart. He either heard Miss Chaworth say to her maid, or was told she had said, "Do you think I could care anything for that lame boy?" This speech, as he himself describes it, was like a shot through his heart. With the summer holidays ended this dream of his youth. He saw Miss Chaworth once more in the succeeding year, and took his last farewell of her, (as he himself used to relate), on that hill near Annesley, which, in his poem of *The Dream*, he describes so happily, as "Crowned with a peculiar diadem." No one, he declared, could have told how much he felt; for his countenance was calm, and his feelings restrained.

The character which Byron bore among the masters on his return to Harrow, was that of an idle boy, who would never learn anything; "and so far as regarded his tasks in school," adds his biographer, "this reputation, by his own avowal, was not ill founded. It is impossible, indeed, to look through the books which he had then in use, and which are scribbled over with clumsy interlined translations, without being struck with the narrow extent of his classical attainments."

The vacation of 1804 he passed with his mother, at Southwell, to which place she had removed from Nottingham, having taken a house on the Green, called Burgage Manor. In the month of October, 1805, he was removed to Trinity College, Cambridge. "When I first went up to college," he says, "it was a new and heavy-hearted scene to me; firstly, I so much disliked leaving Harrow, though it was time, (I being seventeen); it broke my very rest for the last quarter counting the days that remained. Secondly, I wished to go to Oxford, and not to Cambridge. Thirdly, I was so completely alone in this new world, that it half broke my spirits." In the summer of 1806, he, as usual, joined his mother at Southwell; among the small but select society of which place he had, during his visits, formed some intimacies and friendships, which continued long after he had ceased to frequent the place. The family of Pigot, the Rev. John Becher, the Leacrofts, and the Howsons, were principally favoured with his society. One of the most intimate of his friends gives the following account of her first acquaintance with him about this period: "The first time I was introduced to the young Lord Byron was at a party at his mother's house, when he was so shy that she was forced to send for him three times, before she could persuade him to come into the drawing-room to play with the young people at a round game. He was then a fat, bashful boy, with his hair combed straight down his forehead." His visit to Southwell, this summer, was interrupted about the beginning of August, by one of those explosions of temper on the part of Mrs. Byron, to which, from his earliest childhood, he had been but too well accustomed; and in producing which his own rebellious spirit was not always, it may be supposed, entirely blameless. Between a temper at all resembling that of the young Byron, and the loud hurricane bursts of his mother, the collision, it may be supposed, was not a little formidable; and the age at which the son was now arrived, would but render the occasions for such shocks the more frequent. It is told, as a curious proof of their opinion of each other's violence, that, after parting one evening, in a tempest of this kind, they were known each to go privately, that night, to the shop of an apothecary, enquiring anxiously whether the other had been to purchase poison, and cautioning the vendor of drugs not to attend to such an application if made. The disturbance between mother and son, on the occasion above referred to, arose to such a height, that Mrs. Byron aimed a blow at the young lord with the poker, that but for his hasty escape from the parlour, to the house of a friend, might have robbed the world of the glory of *Childe Harold*. Not choosing to return home again, he immediately proceeded to Newark, and took advantage of the earliest coach to London; from which, a day or two afterwards, he despatched a letter, of which the following is a copy, to his friend Pigot, a young gentleman about the same age as himself, in answer to one he had received, apparently by the following post after his flight, giving him some account of the way in which Mrs. Byron had been affected by the conduct of her son.

"16, Piccadilly, August 9, 1806.

"MY DEAR PIGOT,

"Many thanks to you for your *amusing* narrative of the late proceedings of * * * who now begins to feel the effects of her folly. I have just received a penitential epistle; to which, apprehensive of pursuit, I have despatched a moderate answer, with a *kind* of promise to return in a fortnight; this however, (entre nous) I never mean to fulfil. Seriously, your mother has laid me under great obligations; and you, with the rest of your family, merit my warmest thanks for your kind connivance at my escape. * * * * All Southwell, without doubt, is involved in amazement. Apropos—how does my blue-eyed nun, the fair * * * ? Is she *rob'd in sable garb of woe?* Here I remain a week or ten days; previous to my departure you shall receive my address, but what it will be I have not determined. My lodgings must be kept secret from Mrs. B. You may present my compliments to her, and say, any attempt to pursue me will fail. Without doubt, the dames of Southwell reprobate the pernicious example I have shown, and tremble lest their babes should disobey their mandates, and quit in dudgeon their mammas on any grievance. * * * * *

"BYRON."

The following was sent the day after to Miss * * *

"London, August 10, 1806.

"MY DEAR BRIDGET,

"As I have already troubled your brother with more than he will find pleasure in deciphering, you are the next to whom I shall assign the employment of perusing this second epistle. You will perceive from my first, that no idea of Mrs. B's. arrival had disturbed me at the time it was written; *not* so the present, since the appearance of a note from the *illustrious cause* of my *sudden decampment*, has driven the 'natural ruby from my cheeks,' and completely blanched my woe-begone countenance. This gunpowder intimation of her arrival, breathes less of terror and dismay than you will perhaps imagine, and concludes with the comfortable assurance that all *present motion* being prevented by the fatigues of her journey, for which my *blessings* are due to the rough roads, and restive quadrupeds of his majesty's highways. As I have not the smallest intention to be chased round the country, I shall e'en make a merit of necessity; and since, like Macbeth, 'they've tied me to the stake, I cannot fly,' I shall imitate that valorous tyrant, and 'bear-like fight the course,'—all escape being precluded. I can now engage her with less disadvantage, having drawn the enemy from her intrenchments. I shall remain in town for, at least, a week, and expect to hear from *you* before its expiration. Addio! Now to encounter my Hydra.

"Yours ever."

Whatever might be the faults of Mrs. Byron, after all she had suffered from her connexion with his family, nothing could justify her son in speaking of her in this disrespectful manner.

The opinion entertained, at this time, by the young lord, of the population of Nottingham, may be inferred from a passage in a letter to his friend Pigot, where he is complaining bitterly of his servant not arriving at London with his horses; in which he says—"Dear Pigot, forgive this *petulant* effusion, and attribute it to the idle conduct of that precious rascal Charles, who, instead of obeying my instructions, is sauntering through the streets of that *Political Pandemonium, Nottingham.*"

Mr. Pigot, being requested by the biographer to furnish him with a few particulars respecting a journey he made with Lord Byron to Harrowgate, writes as follows:

"We, I remember, went in Lord Byron's own carriage, with post-horses; and he sent his groom with saddled horses, and a beautifully formed very ferocious bull-dog, called Nelson, to meet us there. Boatswain went by the side of his valet, Frank, on the box with us. The bull-dog, Nelson, always wore a muzzle, and was occasionally sent for into our private room, when the muzzle was taken off, much to my annoyance, and he and his master amused themselves with throwing the room into disorder. There was always a jealous feud between this Nelson and Boatswain; and whenever the latter came into the room, while the former was there, they instantly seized each other; and then Byron, myself and Frank, and all the waiters that could be found, were vigorously engaged in parting them, which was in general only effected by thrusting poker and tongues into the mouths of each. But Nelson one day, unfortunately, escaped out of the room without his muzzle, and going into the stable-yard, fastened upon the throat of a horse, from which he could not be disengaged. The stable-boys ran in alarm to find Frank, who, taking one of his lordship's pistols, always kept loaded in his room, shot poor Nelson through the head, to the great regret of Byron."

The small volume of poems which he had now for some time been preparing, was, in the month of November, this year (1806), ready to deliver to the select few among whom it was intended to circulate; and to Mr. Becher the first copy of the work was presented. The whole of this edition, immediately on being received from the press, was, at the instigation of Mr. Becher, burned, in consequence of the loose, or rather, lewd nature, of one or two of the pieces.

Byron was now, during a short stay at Southwell, much

engaged with a company of young amateur performers, in carrying on the amusement of private theatricals. "As his visits to Southwell were," says Moore, "but few and transient, I shall take the present opportunity of mentioning such miscellaneous particulars respecting his habits and modes of life while there, as I have been able to collect. Though so remarkably shy, when he first went to Southwell, his reserve, as he grew more acquainted with the young people of the place, wore off; till, at length, he became a frequenter of their dinner parties and assemblies, and even felt mortified if he heard of a rout to which he was not invited. His horror, however, at new faces still continued; and if, while at Mr. Pigot's, he saw strangers approaching the house, he would instantly even jump out of the window to avoid them. This natural shyness concurred, with no small degree of pride, to keep him aloof from the acquaintance of the gentlemen in the neighbourhood, whose visits, in more than one instance, be left unreturned. The true reason of the haughty distance at which, both now, and afterwards, he stood apart from his more opulent neighbours, is to be found in his mortifying consciousness of the inadequacy of his own means to his rank, and the proud dread of being made to feel his inferiority, by persons to whom, in every other respect, he considered himself to be superior."

Whilst at Southwell, Byron, in one of his playful moods, wrote an "Epitaph on John Adams, of Southwell, a carrier, who died of drunkenness," of which the following is a copy:

"John Adams lies here, of the parish of Southwell,
A *carrier*, who *carried* his can to his mouth well;
He *carried* so much, and he *carried* so fast,
He could *carry* no more, so he's *carried* at last;
For the liquor he drank being too much for one,
He could *carry* no more, so he's now *carri*-on."

Notwithstanding his frequent visits to Southwell, and the kind and friendly manner in which he was treated by many of its respectable inhabitants, he appears to have entertained the deepest dislike, not to say perfect abhorrence, of the whole place. Writing to Dr. Pigot, in April, 1807, he says,—"I shall most probably be in Essex, or London, when you arrive at this d—d place." On his arrival at Cambridge, in June, the same year, he writes thus to Miss ——: "Some say I look *better* than when I was last here, some *worse*, but all agree I am *thinner*—more I do not require. I have lost ten pounds in weight since I left your cursed, detestable, and abhorred abode of scandal; where, excepting yourself and John Becher, I care not if the whole race were consigned to the pit of Acheron, which I would visit in person, rather than contaminate my sandals with the polluted dust of Southwell. Seriously, unless obliged, by the emptiness of my purse, to re-visit Mrs. B., you will see me no more."

The following extract will show the manner in which his lordship passed most of his time at college:

"The Marquis of Tavistock was down the other day; I supped with him at his tutor's—entirely a Whig party. The opposition muster strongly here now, and Lord Hartington, the Duke of Leinster, &c., are to join us in October, so everything will be *splendid*. Met with another *accidency;* upset a butter-boat in the lap of a lady—look'd very *blue*—spectators grinned—curse 'em! *Apropos*, sorry to say, been *drunk* every day, and not quite *sober* yet. However, touch no meat, nothing but fish, soup, and vegetables, consequently it does me no harm. Sad dogs all the *Cantabs*. This place is a *monotony of endless variety*—like it—hate Southwell. Has Ridge sold well? (his volume of poems) or do the ancients demur? Saw a lady at St. Mary's the image of Anne ****, thought it was her; all in the wrong. The lady stared, so did I; I *blushed*, so did *not* the lady. Sad thing; wish women had *more modesty*. Talking of women, puts me in mind of my terrier Fanny—how is she? Got a head-ache; must go to bed; up early in the morning to travel. Mem. *I hate Southwell.*"

Another choice specimen or two of his lordship's correspondence with Miss ——, of Southwell:

"The intelligence of London cannot be interesting to you, who have rusticated all your life; the annals of routs, riots, balls, and boxing-matches, cards and crim. con., masquerades, mechanics, Argyle Institution and aquatic races, love and lotteries, Brookes's and Buonaparte, opera-singers and oratorios, wine, women, waxwork, and weather-cocks, can't agree with your insulated ideas of decorum, and other silly expressions not inserted in our vocabulary. Oh! Southwell, Southwell, how I rejoice to have left thee, and how I curse the many hours I dragged along, for so many months, among the Mohawks who inhabit your kraals!"

"Trinity College, Cambridge, Oct. 26, 1807.

"My Dear Elizabeth—Fatigued with sitting up till four in the morning, for the last two days, at hazard, I take up my pen to inquire how your highness, and the rest of my female acquaintances at the seat of archiepiscopal grandeur, go on. I know I deserve a scolding for my negligence, in not writing more frequently; but racing up and down the country, for these last three months, how was it possible to fulfil the duties of a correspondent? Fixed, at last, for six weeks, I write, as *thin* as ever, (not having gained an ounce since my reduction) and rather in better humour; but, after all, Southwell was a detestable residence. Thank St. Dominica, I have done with it; I have been twice within eight miles of it, but could not prevail on myself to *suffocate* in its heavy atmosphere. This place is wretched enough—a villainous chaos of din and drunkenness; nothing but hazard and Burgundy, hunting, mathematics, and Newmarket riot and racing. Oh! the misery of doing nothing but make *love, enemies*, and *verses.* I have got a new friend, the finest in the world—*a tame bear.* When I bought him here, they asked me what I meant to do with him, and my reply was, 'he should *sit for a fellowship.*' This answer delighted them not. We have several parties here; and this evening a large assortment of jockeys, gamblers, boxers, authors, parsons, and poets, sup with me—a precious mixture, but they go on well together."

"It is but rarely," says Lord Byron's biographer, "that infidelity, or scepticism, finds an entrance into youthful minds. Their readiness to take the future upon trust, which is the charm of this period of life, would naturally, indeed, make it the season of belief, as well as of hope. Unfortunately, Lord Byron was an exception to this rule. With him the canker showed itself 'in the morn and dew of youth,' when the effect of such 'blastments' is, for every reason, most fatal; and in addition to the real misfortune of being an unbeliever at any age, he exhibited the rare and melancholy spectacle of an unbelieving school-boy. The same premature development which brought his passions and genius so early into action, enabled him also to anticipate this worst, dreariest result of reason; and at the very time of life when a spirit and temperament like his most required control, those checks which religious prepossessions best supply, were almost wholly wanting. After his departure from Southwell, he had not a single friend or relative to whom he could look up with respect, but was thrown alone on the world, with his passions and his pride, to revel in the fatal discovery, which he imagined himself to have made, of the nothingness of the future, and the all paramount claims of the present. By singular ill fortune, too, the individual who, among all his college friends, had taken the strongest hold on his admiration and affection, and whose loss he afterwards lamented with brotherly tenderness, was, to the same extent as himself, if not more strongly, a sceptic. Writing of this friend, some time after his death, he says—'Matthews and I, meeting in London, and elsewhere, became great cronies. He was not good tempered; nor am I; but with a little tact, his temper was manageable; and I thought him so superior a man, that I was willing to sacrifice something to his humours, which were often, at the same time, amusing and provoking. We went down to Newstead together, where I had got a famous cellar, and monks dresses, from a masqerade warehouse. We were a company of some seven or eight, with an occasional neighbour or so for visitors, and used to sit up late in our friars' dresses, drinking Burgundy, claret, champagne, and what not, out of the *skull-cup,* and all sorts of glasses, and buffooning all round the house in our conventual garments. Matthews always denominated me the *Abbot,* and never called me by any other name, in his good humours, to the day of his death.' As already, before his acquaintance with Mr. Matthews, (who was likewise the special bosom friend of Mr. Hobhouse) Lord Byron had begun to bewilder himself in the mazes of scepticism, it would be unjust to impute to this gentleman any further share in the formation of his noble friend's opinions than what arose from the natural influence of example and sympathy—an influence which, as it was felt, perhaps, equally on both sides, rendered the contagion of their doctrines in a great measure reciprocal."

In the early part of 1808 came out the celebrated criticism of the *Edinburgh Review* on his *Hours of Idleness.* "The effect this criticism produced upon his lordship," Moore says, "can only be conceived by those who can understand all that there was in the temper and disposition of Lord Byron, to make him feel it with tenfold more acuteness than others. We have seen with what feverish anxiety he awaited the verdicts of all the minor reviews, and, from his sensibility to praise of the meanest of these censors, we may guess how painfully he must have writhed under the sneers of the highest. A friend, who found him in the first moments of excitement, after reading the article, (during which time he himself says he drank *three bottles of claret*) inquired anxiously whether he had just received a challenge? not knowing how else to account for the fierce defiance of his looks."

It was in the autumn of 1808 that Byron, for the first time, really took up his *residence* at Newstead—Lord Grey de Ruthven having left it a few months before. On the 12th of October, his lordship, as it would seem from a letter to his mother, dated from Newstead, attended a ball at Nottingham, for the benefit of the General Hospital. The passage alluded to runs thus: "As I have a friend here, we will go to the Infirmary Ball on the 12th: we will drink tea with Mrs. Byron at eight o'clock, and expect to see you at the ball. If that lady will allow us a couple of rooms to dress in, we shall be highly obliged. If we are not at the ball till ten or eleven it will be time enough, and we shall return to Newstead about three or four." In a letter during the spring of this year, to Mr. Becher, of Southwell, he says: "*Entre nous,* I am cursedly dipped; my debts, everything inclusive, will be nine or ten thousand before I am twenty-one."

The sort of life which Byron led at this period, between the dissipations of London and of Cambridge, without a home to welcome, or even the roof of a single relative to receive him, was but little calculated to render him satisfied either with himself or the world. Unrestricted, as he was, by any will but his own, even the pleasures to which he was naturally most inclined palled upon him, for want of those best zests of all enjoyment, rarity and restraint. In a passage in one of his note-books, in which is a description of his feelings on first going to Cambridge, he says, "One of the deadliest and heaviest feelings of my life was to feel that I was no longer a boy." "From that moment," he adds, "I began to grow old in my own esteem, and in my esteem age is not estimable. I took my gradations in the vices with great promptitude, but they were not to my taste; for my early passions, though violent in the extreme, were concentrated, and hated division, or spreading abroad. I could have left, or lost, the whole world with, or for, that which I loved; but though my temperament was naturally burning, I could not share in the common-place libertinism of the place without disgust. And yet this very disgust, and my heart thrown back upon itself, threw me into excesses, perhaps more fatal than those from which I shrunk, as fixing upon one (at a time) the passions which spread amongst many would have hurt only myself."

The following amour, if such a degrading association is worthy of being dignified by that name, was indulged in by his lordship, then just of age: A young female, of loose character, with whom he became acquainted, was not only allowed openly to domesticate herself with him in lodgings, at Brompton, but he also allowed her to accompany him, disguised in boy's clothes, to Brighton, where she used to ride about with him in male attire, and was introduced to several persons, strangers to his family connexions, as a younger brother.

During his stay at Brighton, Jackson, the gentleman pugilist, and great patron of "the ring," at this time, was one of his most constant visitors—the travelling expenses of *the professor*, thither and back again, being always defrayed by his lordship. For this person, who he styled his "old friend, and corporeal pastor and master," he continued throughout life to entertain the sincerest regard. On his return to Nottinghamshire, his lordship, on the 4th October, wrote to Mr. Jackson as follows: "I should be very glad to see you here, but the house is filled with workpeople, and undergoing a thorough repair. I hope, however, to be more fortunate before many months have elapsed."

His time at Newstead, during this autumn, was principally occupied in preparing his *Satire* for the press. It is somewhat remarkable that, excited as he was by the attack of the reviewers, and possessing, at all times, such rapid powers of composition, he should have allowed so long an interval to elapse between the aggression and the revenge: but he seemed to consider that his chances of future eminence in literature, of which he had now become really ambitious, depended upon the effort he was about to make, and therefore deliberately collected all his energies for the spring. The misanthropic mood of mind into which he was now beginning to fall, from thwarted hopes and disappointed affections, made the character of satirist perfectly welcome to his craving spirit.

His coming of age, in 1809, was celebrated at Newstead by such festivities as his narrow means and society would allow. Of Lord Byron's own method of commemorating the day, he gives the following curious record, in a letter written from Genoa, in 1822: "Did I ever tell you," he says, "that the day I came of age I dined on eggs and bacon, and a bottle of ale? For once in a way they are my favourite dish and drinkable; but as neither of them agree with me, I never use them but on great jubilees—once in four or five years, or so."

The pecuniary supplies necessary towards his outset, at this epoch, appear to have been procured from money-lenders, at an enormously usurious interest, the payment of which, for a long time, continued to be a burden to him.

In a letter to Mrs. Byron, (his mother) dated March 6th, 1809, there occurs the following remarkable passage in reference to Newstead: "What you say is all very true: come what may, *Newstead and I stand or fall together*. I have now lived on the spot, I have fixed my heart upon it, and no pressure, present or future, shall induce me to barter the last vestige of our inheritance. I have that pride within me which will enable me to support difficulties. I can endure privations; but could I obtain in exchange for Newstead Abbey the first fortune in the country, I would reject the proposition. Set your mind at ease, therefore, on that score; Mr. H** talks like a man of business on the subject—I feel like a man of honour, and *will not sell Newstead*. I shall get my seat on the return of the affidavits from Cornwall, and will do something in the House soon; I must dash, or it is all over. My *Satire* must be kept secret for a month, after that you may say what you please on the subject."

The *Satire* was published early in March, and his lordship took his seat in the House of Lords on the 13th of the same month. "On that day," says Mr. Dallas, "passing down St. James's-street, but with no intention of calling, I saw his chariot at his door, and went in. His countenance, paler than usual, showed that his mind was agitated He said to me, 'I am glad you happened to come in; I am going to take my seat, perhaps you will go with me.' I expressed my readiness to attend him; while, at the same time, I concealed the shock I felt that this young man, who by birth, fortune, and talent, stood high in life, should have lived so unconnected and neglected by persons of his own rank, that there was not a single member of the senate to which he belonged to whom he could, or would, apply to introduce him in a manner becoming his birth. I saw that he felt the situation, and I fully partook of his indignation. After some talk about the *Satire*, the last sheets of which were in the press, I accompanied Lord Byron to the House. He was received in one of the ante-chambers by an officer in attendance, with whom he settled respecting the fees he had to pay. One of them then went to apprise the Lord-Chancellor of his being there, and soon returned for him. When his lordship entered, I thought he looked still paler than before; and he certainly wore a countenance in which mortification was mingled with, but subdued by, indignation. He passed the woolsack without looking round, and advanced to the table where the proper officer was attending to administer the oaths. When he had gone through them, the Chancellor quitted his seat, and went towards him with a smile, putting out his hand warmly to welcome him; and though I did not catch his words, I saw that he paid him some compliment. This was all thrown away upon Byron, who made a stiff bow, and put the tips of his fingers into his lordship's hand. The Chancellor, of course, did not press a welcome so received, but resumed his seat; whilst Lord Byron carelessly seated himself for a few moments on one of the empty benches to the left of the throne, usually occupied by the lords in opposition. When, on his joining me, I expressed what I had felt, he said—'If I had shaken hands heartily, he would have set me down for one of his party; but I will have nothing to do with any of them on either side! I have taken my seat, and now I will go abroad.' "

The slights to which Byron, at this period, was exposed, and which, it is fair to assume, were but the results of that unenviable notoriety he had obtained by the profligacy of his principles and conduct, among all persons who felt that they had a character to lose, excited in him, at times, the most painful and irritative feelings. Mr. Dallas, who witnessed the result of one of these *cold-shoulder* receptions of his lordship, by a gentleman, a former college friend, and whose acquaintanceship he was then desirous of renewing, thus describes its effect upon him: "I found him," he says, "bursting with indignation. 'Will you believe it' said he, 'I have just met ***, and asked him to come in and sit an hour with me. He excused himself: and what do you think was his excuse? *He was engaged with his mother, and some ladies, to go shopping!* and he knows I set out to-morrow, to be absent for years, perhaps never to return. Friendship! I do not believe I shall leave behind me, yourself and family excepted, and perhaps my mother, a single being who will care what becomes of me.'"

In a few days after his admission to his seat in the House of Lords, Byron, in disgust with everything, and almost with everybody around him, returned gloomily to the seclusion of Newstead, there to brood, with bitter feelings, over that early, but dear-bought experience of the vanity and worthlessness of all those maddening pleasures to which his life, prematurely, had been so much devoted, or to feed his sickening heart with future visions of joys to be found in those far-off scenes, where he anticipated that his spirit might have more amplitude of space in which to expatiate in the pursuit of pleasure, than he had been able to find in the restricted and conventional society of his native country. It was not long, however, defore he was summoned back to town by the success of his *Satire*, the rapid sale of which had already rendered another edition necessary. Whilst engaged in preparing this new edition for the press, he was also gaily dispensing the hospitalities of Newstead to a party of young college friends, whom, with the prospect of a long absence from England, he had assembled round him at the Abbey, for a sort of festive farewell. The following letter from one of the party, (Mr. Charles Skinner Matthews) before alluded to, as a picture taken freshly, and at the moment, of a scene so pregnant with character, will no doubt be highly acceptable to the visitor to Newstead. The letter is dated

London, May 22, 1809.

My Dear——, I must begin with giving you a few particulars of the singular place I have latterly quitted. Newstead Abbey is situate 130 miles from London—four on this side Mansfield. It is so fine a piece of antiquity, that I should think there must be a description, and perhaps a picture of it, in *Grose*. The ancestors of its present owner came into possession of it at the time of the dissolution of the monasteries, but the building itself is of a much earlier date. Though sadly fallen into decay, it is still completely an *Abbey*, and most part of it is still standing in the same style as when it was first built. There are two tiers of cloisters, with a variety of cells and rooms about them, which, though not inhabited, nor in an habitable state, might easily be made so; and many of the original rooms, among which is a fine stone hall, are still in use. Of the Abbey church, only one end remains; and the old kitchen, with a long range of apartments, is reduced to a heap of rubbish. Leading from the Abbey to the modern part of the habitation is a noble room, about seventy feet in length, and twenty-three in breadth; but every part of the house displays neglect and decay, save those which the present lord has lately fitted up. The house and gardens are entirely surrounded by a wall, with battlements. In front is a large lake, bordered here and there with castellated buildings, the chief of which stands on an eminence at the further extremity of it. Fancy all this surrounded with bleak and barren hills, with scarce a tree to be seen for miles, except a solitary clump or two, and you will have some idea of Newstead. For the late lord being at enmity with his son, to whom the estate was secured by entail, resolved, out of spite to the same, that the estate should descend to him in as miserable plight as he could possibly reduce it to; for which cause he took no care of the mansion, and fell to lopping of every tree he could lay his hand on, so furiously, that he reduced immense tracts of woodland country to the desolate state I have just described. However, his son died before him, so that all his rage was thrown away. So much for the place, concerning which I have thrown together these few particulars, meaning my account to be, like the place itself, without any or derro connection. Ascend then, with me, the hall steps, that I may introduce you to my lord and his visitants. But have a care how you proceed; be mindful to go there in broad daylight, and with your eyes about you; for should you make any blunder,—should you go to the right of the hall steps, you are laid hold of by a bear; and should you go to the left, the case is still worse, for you run full against a wolf! Nor when you have attained the door is your danger over; for the hall being decayed, and therefore standing in need of repair, a bevy of inmates are very probably banging at one end of it with their pistols; so that if you enter without giving loud notice of your approach, you have only escaped the wolf and the bear to expire by the pistol shots of the merry monks of Newstead. Our party consisted of Lord Byron, and four or five others, and was now and then increased by the presence of a neighbouring parson. As for our way of living, the order of the day was generally this: for breakfast we had no set hour, but each suited his own convenience—everything remaining on the table till the whole party had done; though had one wished to breakfast at the early hour of ten, he would have been rather lucky to find any of the servants up. Our average time of rising was about *one*. I, who generally got up between eleven and twelve, was always, even when an invalid, the first of the party, and was esteemed a prodigy of early rising. It was frequently past two before the breakfast party broke up. Then, for the amusement of the morning, there was reading, fencing, single-stick, or shuttlecock, in the great room; practising with pistols, in the hall; walking, riding, cricket, sailing on the lake, playing with the bear, or teasing the wolf. Between seven and eight we dined; and our evening lasted from that time till one, two, or three in the morning. The evening diversions may be easily conceived. I must not omit the custom of handing round, after dinner, on the removal of the cloth, a human skull, filled with burgundy. After revelling on choice viands, and the finest wines of France, we adjourned to tea, where we amused ourselves with reading, or improving conversation, each according to his fancy, and, after sandwiches, &c., retired to rest. A set of monkish dresses,, which had been provided with all the proper apparatus of *crosses, beads, tonsure,* &c., often gave a variety to our appearance and our pursuits."

That gaming was among his follies, at this period, he himself tells us, in his journal. "Gamesters," he says, "I have a notion are as happy as many people, being always *excited.* Women, wine, fame, the table—even ambition *sate* now and then; but every turn of the card, and cast of the dice, keeps the gamester alive: besides, one can game ten times longer than one can do anything else. I was very fond of it when young, (he was not of age when this was written) that is to say, of hazard, for I hate all card games, even faro. When macco (or whatever they spell it) was introduced, I gave up the whole thing; for I loved, and missed, the rattle of the box and dice, and the glorious uncertainty, not only of good luck or bad luck, but of *any luck* at all, as one had sometimes to throw often to decide at all. I have thrown as many as fourteen mains running, and carried of all the cash upon the table occasionally; but I had no coolness, or judgment, or calculation. It was the delight, the excitement of the thing, that pleased me. Upon the whole, I left off in time, without being much a winner or loser."

Among the causes—if not rather among the results—of that disposition to melancholy, which, after all, perhaps, naturally belonged to his temperament, must not be forgotten those sceptical views of religion which clouded, as has been shown, his boyish thoughts; "and at the time," says Mr. Moore, "of which I am speaking, gathered still more darkly over his mind. In general, we find the young too ardently occupied with the enjoyments which this life gives, or promises, to afford either leisure or inclination for much inquiry into the mysteries of the next. But with him, unfortunately, it was otherwise; and to have, at once, anticipated the worst experience both of the voluptuary and the reasoner—to have reached, as he supposed, the boundary of this world's pleasures, and see nothing but clouds and darkness beyond, was the doom, the anomalous doom, which a nature, premature in all its passions and powers, inflicted on Lord Byron."

Having put the finishing hand to the new edition of his *Satire*, he, without waiting for the fresh honours that were in store for him, took leave of London (whither he had returned from Nottinghamshire) on the 11th of June, 1809, and in about a fortnight after, in company with his friend Hobhouse, sailed for Lisbon.

At the conclusion of a letter he wrote to his friend Hodgson, dated Falmouth, June 25th, 1809, he says: "I don't know when I can write again, because it depends on that experienced navigator, Captain Kidd, and the 'stormy winds that (don't) blow' at this season. I leave England without regret—I shall return to it without pleasure. I am like Adam, the first convict, sentenced to transportation, but I have no Eve, and have eaten no apple, but what was sour as a crab; and thus ends my first chapter. Adieu."

In another letter to Mr. Hodgson, dated *Salsette* frigate, in the Dardanelles, May 5th, 1810, he writes thus: "We have undergone some inconveniences, and incurred partial perils, but no events worthy of communicating, unless you will deem it one that, two days ago, I swam from Sestos to Abydos. This, with a few alarms from robbers, and some danger of shipwreck in a Turkish galliot, six months ago, a visit to a Pacha, a passion for a married woman at Malta, a challenge to an officer, an attachment to three Greek girls, sisters, for whom I am dying for love, though all of them are under fifteen, a great deal of buffoonery, and fine prospects—form all that has distinguished my progress since my departure from Spain." At the termination of this epistle he indulges in the following strain of mock humility, or repentance, for his past follies: "I hope you will find me an altered personage—I do not mean in body, but in manners—for I begin to find out that nothing will do in this d—d world but virtue. I am tolerably sick of vice, which I have tried in all its agreeable varieties, and mean, on my return, to cut off all my dissolute acquaintance, leave off wine and carnal company, and betake myself to politics and decorum. I am very serious and cynical, and a good deal disposed to moralise, but, fortunately for you, the coming homily is cut short by default of pen and defection of paper."

A letter to Mrs. Byron, dated Athens, February 28th, 1811, contains some interesting remarks respecting Newstead, and his future prospects in life:

> "DEAR MADAM—As I have received a firman for Egypt, &c., I shall proceed to that quarter in the spring, and I beg you will state to Mr. H. that it is necessary to have further remittances. On the subject of Newstead, I answer as before, *No.* If it is necessary to sell, sell Rochdale. Fletcher will have arrived by this time with my letters to that effect. I will tell you fairly, I have, in the first place, no opinion of funded property; if by any particular circumstances I shall be led to adopt such a determination, I will, at all events, pass my life abroad, as my only tie to England is Newstead, and that once gone, neither interest nor inclination lead me northward. * * * * This, then, is the alternative—if I preserve Newstead, I return; if I sell it, stay away."

In June, 1811, his lordship appears to have made up his mind to return to England, after having been absent just two years. This step was, perhaps, as much the result of necessity as of choice; his whole affairs were in a condition of complete disorganization, and his presence at home appears to have been absolutely necessary, even for an attempt at their adjustment.

In a letter dated at sea, June 29th, 1811, he thus writes to Mr. Hodgson: "In a week, with a fair wind, we shall be in Portsmouth, and on the 2nd of July I shall have completed (to a day) two years of peregrination, from which I am returning with as little emotion as I set out. Indeed, my prospects are not very pleasant; embarassed in my private affairs; indifferent to public; solitary, without the wish to be social; with a body a little enfeebled by a succession of fevers, but a spirit, I trust, unbroken, I am returning home without a hope, and almost without a desire. The first thing I shall have to encounter will be a lawyer, the next a creditor; then colliers, farmers, surveyors, and all the agreeable attachments to estates out of repair, and contested coal-pits. In short, I am sick and sorry, and when I have a little repaired my irreparable affairs, away I shall march either to campaign in Spain, or back again to the East, where I can at least have cloudless skies, and a cessation from impertinence."

In a letter to Mr. Dallas, a few days before his arrival in England, his lordship says: "I am coming back with little prospect of pleasure at home, and with a body a little shaken by one or two smart fevers, but a spirit, I hope, yet unbroken. My affairs, it seems, are considerably involved; and much business must be done with lawyers, creditors, colliers, and farmers. Now this, to a man who hates bustle as he hates a bishop, is a serious concern. But enough of my home department."

Immediately on Lord Byron's arrival in London, Mr. Dallas called upon him. "On the 15th of July," says this gentleman, "I had the pleasure of shaking hands with him at Reddish's Hotel, in St. James's-street. He was very animated in the account of his travels, but assured me he never had any idea of writing them."

On looking over a large packet of papers, principally consisting of poetry, which had been confided to his inspection by Lord Byron, Mr. Dallas found the first Canto of *Childe Harold's Pilgrimage.* In reference to this poem, his lordship said, "The verses had been read but by one person, who found very little to commend, and much to condemn; that he himself was of that opinion, and he was sure I should be so too." The value of the treasure thus presented to him, Mr. Dallas was not slow in discovering. That very evening he despatched a letter to his noble friend, saying: "You have written one of the most delightful poems I ever read. I have been so fascinated with *Childe Harold,* that I have not been able to lay it down. I would almost pledge my life on its advancing the reputation of your poetical powers, and on gaining you great honour and regard, if you will do me the credit, and favour of attending to my suggesstions respecting," &c., &c. Mr. Dallas, after some delay, having at length overcome his lordship's scruples respecting his poems, though he said, again and again, that he "was going to get him into a scrape with his old enemies, and that none of them would rejoice more than the *Edinburgh Reviewers* at an opportunity to humble him," the poem was sent to press; and, as is well known, realized the most sanguine expectations of his friends in its reception by the public.

While thus busily engaged in his literary projects, and having, besides, some law affairs to transact with his agent, he was called suddenly away to Newstead, by the intelligence of an event which seems, at this time, to have effected his mind far more deeply than, considering all the circumstances of the case, might have been expected: this was the sudden and alarming illness of his mother, who expired on the 1st of August. Mrs. Byron had been ill for a short time, but no particular danger was apprehended; a fit of passion, however, brought on a crisis, from which she never rallied. Though no such feeling had hardly ever, since infancy, or early boyhood, subsisted between Lord Byron and his mother, as usually characterizes that tender relationship of mother and child, he almost uniformly in his letters addressing her as "Mrs. Byron," or "Madam," yet the stroke of final separation seemed, for awhile, to affect him a good deal. He declined, however, to accompany the corpse to its resting-place, but stood at the Abbey door, looking at the procession till it moved off; then turning to young Rushton, the constant attendant and sharer in all his athletic exercises, who was the only person left in the house, besides himself, he desired him to fetch the sparring-gloves, and proceeded to his usual exercises with the young man: but after a brief period of bodily exertion in this way, indulged in, probably, as much to stifle emotion as for amusement, he flung away the gloves, and retired to his chamber.

A letter from his lordship to Mr. Bolton, his solicitor at Nottingham, dated Newstead Abbey, August, 20th, 1811, respecting that clause in his will, whereby he directed that "his carcase," should be interred in the vault he had prepared beside his dog Boatswain, contains the following passage: "I forgot to mention that it must be specified by codicil, or otherwise, that my body is, on no account, to be removed from the vault where I have directed it to be placed; and in case any of my successors, within the entail, (from bigotry or otherwise) might think proper to remove the carcase, such proceedings shall be attended by forfeiture of the estate;

which, in such case, shall go to my sister, the Hon. Augusta Leigh, and her heirs, on similar conditions."

It is a somewhat remarkable circumstance, that Byron could not prevail on any of his literary friends to form the same estimate of the genius of Henry Kirke White, which himself entertained. Writing to Mr. Dallas, from Newstead, August 21st, he says: "I am sorry you don't like Harry White; with a great deal of cant, which in him was sincere, (indeed it killed him) *certes*, there is poetry and genius. * * * It is astonishing how little he was known; and at Cambridge no one heard or thought of such a man, till his death rendered all notice useless. For my own part, I should have been most proud of such an acquaintance—his very prejudices were respectable."

The unfortunate condition of his lordship's mind, during his residence at Newstead, this year (1811), a condition which he really never made a rally to overcome, by forming any high, or noble resolve, that was in just accordance with his talents, and the responsibility to which, as a rational and accountable creature, he could not, in moments of serious reflection, but feel himself to be liable, is painfully apparent in the terms of the following letter, addressed to Mr. Hodgson:

"Newstead Abbey, Oct. 13, 1811.

* * * * * * *

"I am growing *nervous*, (how you will laugh) but it is true—really, wretchedly, ridiculously, fine lady-cally *nervous*. Your climate kills me. I can neither read, nor write, nor amuse myself, nor any one else. My days are listless, and my nights restless; I have very seldom any society, when I have, I run out of it. At 'this present writing,' there are three ladies, and I have stolen away to write this grumbling letter. I don't know that I shan't end with insanity, for I find a want of method in arranging my thoughts that perplexes me strangely; but this looks more like silliness than madness, as Scrope Davis would facetiously remark in his consoling manner. 'I have almost forgot the taste of grief,' and 'supped full of horrors,' till I have become callous, nor have I a tear left for an event which, five years ago, would have bowed down my head to the earth. It seems as though I were to experience in my youth the greatest misery of age. My friends fall around me, and I shall be left a lonely tree before I am withered. Other men can always take refuge in their families; I have no resource but in my own reflections, and they present no prospect, here or hereafter, except the selfish satisfaction of surviving my betters. I am, indeed, very wretched, and you will excuse my saying so, as you know I am not apt to cant of sensibility."

At the same date with this melancholy letter, is a copy of verses, in answer to a friend, who exhorted him to be cheerful, and "banish care," introduced as follows:

> "Oh! banish care—such ever be
> The motto of *thy* revelry!
> Perchance of mine, when wassail nights
> Renew those riotous delights,
> Wherewith the children of despair
> Lull the lorn heart, and 'banish care,'
> But not in morn's reflecting hour,
> When present, past, and future lower,
> When all I loved is changed or gone,
> Mock with such taunts the woes of one,
> Whose every thought—but let them pass—
> Thou knows't I am not what I was.
> But above all, if thou would'st hold
> Place in a heart that ne'er was cold,
> By all the powers that men revere,
> By all unto thy bosom dear,
> Thy joys below, thy hopes above,
> Speak—speak of any thing but love."

* * * * *

On the 27th of February, 1812, a day or two before the appearance of *Childe Harold*, Lord Byron made the first trial of his eloquence in the House of Lords. The subject of debate was the "Nottingham Frame-breaking Bill;" and Lord Byron having mentioned to Mr. Rogers his intention to take part in the discussion, a communication was, by the intervention of that gentleman, opened between the noble poet and Lord Holland, when several letters passed between them on the subject. On this question Lord Byron made up his mind, as will readily be perceived from the following extract from one of the letters addressed to Lord Holland, to give his strenuous opposition to the proposed measures of the government. "My own motive," says he, "for opposing the bill, is founded on its palpable injustice, and its certain inefficacy. I have seen the state of these miserable men, and it is a disgrace to a civilized country. Their excesses may be condemned, but cannot be subject of wonder. The effect of the present bill would be to drive them into actual rebellion."

His lordship, whilst at Newstead, during the prevalence of the Luddite disturbances, had made several visits to the manufacturing villages in the vicinity of his residence, and attended a meeting of the magistrates, at the County Hall, on the subject of the means to be adopted for the suppression of the outrages; at which meeting, it was stated, that he expressed briefly, but strongly, his opinions against the measures adopted by the government and the magistracy, as well as the manufacturers generally, in reference to these misguided men. Several persons, admirers of his lordship's talents as a poet, were assembled on the High-pavement, near the Hall, to see him pass. He looked on the occasion very well and cheerful, as he passed in conversation with some gentlemen by whom he was accompanied; and though from the mal-formation of one of his feet, somewhat halting in his gait, he had, by the graceful way in which he carried his head, and, indeed, the whole upper part of his frame, an air of self-nobleness which much distinguished him from all around. The reception his lordship met with among the peers, on the delivery of his speech, for which he had prepared himself with great care, was highly flattering; some of the noble speakers, on his own side, complimented him very warmly, and it was evident to every observer, that he was no little pleased and satisfied with himself. His lordship made two or three other attempts at oratory in the House, but they were not distinguished by much success.

Notwithstanding all the declarations and assurances made by Lord Byron to his mother, in 1809, that "come what might, the last vestige of the inheritance of his family, Newstead, should never be parted with by him," at the latter end of this year (1812) it was actually brought to the hammer, but not at that time sold; only £90,000 being offered for the property. It was, however, shortly afterwards sold, by private contract, to T. Claughton, Esq., for £140,000. Byron, in a letter to Moore, about this time, alluding to the impediments which soon were found to arise in the way of Mr. Claughton completing his purchase, says: "This day I have received information from my man of law of the *non*, and never likely to be, performance of purchase by Mr. Claughton, of *im*pecuniary memory. He don't know what to do, or when to pay, and so all my hopes and worldly projects and prospects are gone to the devil. He (the purchaser, to the devil,

too, for aught I care), and I, and my legal advisers, are to meet to-morrow, the said purchaser having first taken special care to enquire 'whether I could meet him with temper?' Certainly. The question is this—shall I either have the estate back, which is as good as ruin, or shall I go on with him dawdling, which is rather worse." Eventually, Mr. Claughton relinquished the bargain and paid forfeit. "Newstead is to be mine again," says his lordship, in a letter to Moore, of the 3rd August, 1814, "Claughton forfeits *twenty-five thousand pounds;* but that don't prevent me from being very prettily ruined. I mean to bury myself there—and let my beard grow—and hate you all."

That peevish, melancholy mood, in which he was apt to indulge, about this time, breaks out very strikingly in a letter written to Mr. Moore, shortly after the one just quoted. "For my own part, I have *seriously* and not *whiningly* (for that is not my way, at least, it used not to be), neither hopes, nor prospects, nor scarcely even wishes. I am, in some respects, happy, but not in a manner that can or ought to *last*—but enough of that. The worst of it is, I feel quite enervated and indifferent. If I was born, as the nurses say, with a silver spoon in my mouth, it has stuck in my throat, and spoiled my palate, so that nothing put into it is swallowed with much relish, unless it be Cayenne. However, I have grievances enough to occupy me that way too. P. S. Don't forget my god-son. You could not have fixed on a fitter porter for his sins than me, being used to carry double, without inconvenience."

Writing to Mr. Rogers, the poet, March 25th, 1813, his lordship says: "I enclose you a draft for the usurious interest due to Lord ——'s *protége*; I also could wish you would state this much for me to his lordship. Though the transaction speaks plainly in itself for the borrower's folly, and the lender's usury, it never was my intention to quash the demand, as I legally might, nor to withhold payment of principal, or, perhaps, unlawful interest. You know what my situation has been, and what it is. I have parted with an estate (which has been in my family for nearly three hundred years, and was never disgraced by being in possession of a *lawyer*, a *churchman*, or a *woman*, during that period) to liquidate this and similar demands; and the payment of the purchase is still withheld, and may be, perhaps, for years. If, therefore, I am under the necessity of making those persons wait for their money, (which, considering the terms, they can afford to suffer,) it is my misfortune."

Mr. Moore having, during the year 1813, taken up his residence at Ashbourne, and being a frequent visitor at the seat of the Earl of Moira, Donnington Park, Lord Byron addressed a letter to him, dated Bennet-street, London, August 22nd, which contained the following passage: "I am now thinking of regretting that, just as I have left Newstead, you reside near it. Did you ever see it? Do; but don't tell me that you like it. If I had known of such intellectual neighbourhood, I don't think I should have quitted it. You could have come over so often as a bachelor—for it was a thorough bachelor's mansion—plenty of wine, and such sordid sensualities, with books enough, room enough, and an air of antiquity about all, (except the lasses) that would have suited you, when pensive, and served you to laugh at when in glee. I had built myself a bath and a vault, and now I shan't even be buried in it. It's odd; but we can't even be certain of a *grave*, at least a particular one."

Even up to this period, his lordship had not lost his predilection for the "fancy," nor his love of the company of a bevy of pugilists assembled around a festive board. At the latter end of this year he attended a meeting of this kind, the particulars of which are thus recorded in his journal: "12, *mezza notte*. Just returned from dinner with Jackson (the emperor of pugilism) and another of the elect, at Crib's, the champion's. I drank more than I like, and have brought away some three bottles of very fair claret—for I have no headache. We had Tom —— up after dinner; very facetious, though somewhat prolix. He don't like his situation—wants to fight again. Pray Pollux (or Castor, if he was the miller,) he may! Tom has been a sailor, a coalheaver, and some other genteel profession, before he took to the cestus. Tom has been in action at sea, and is now only three-and-thirty. A great man! Has a wife and a mistress; and conversations well. Tom is an old friend of mine; I have seen some of his best battles in my nonage. He is now a publican, and I fear, a sinner; for Mrs. —— is an alimony, and ——'s daughter lives with the champion. Tom, having an opinion of my morals, passed her off as a legal spouse. Talking of her, he said 'she was the truest of women,' from which I immediately inferred she could *not* be his wife; and so it turned out."

The following account of his lordship's gastronomic habits are extracted from his journal: "Sunday. I dined with the Lord Holland, in St. James's-square: large party. Stuffed myself with sturgeon, and exceeded in champagne, and wine in general, but not to a confusion of head. When I *do* dine, I gorge like an Arab, or a boa snake, on fish and vegetables, but no meat. I am always better, however, on my tea and biscuit, than on any other regimen, and even that sparingly."

The following extract from his lordship's journal, during the month of March, 1814, will show the desultory way in which he still continued to spend his time, and the unsatisfactory state of his mind in reference to almost every subject: "March 17. I have been sparring with Jackson for exercise this morning, and mean to continue and renew my acquaintance with the mufflers. My chest, and arms, and wind are in very good plight, and I am not in flesh. I used to be a hard hitter, and my arms are very long for my height (5 ft 8½ in.) *Redde the Quarrels of Authors*, (another sort of sparring) a new work, by that most entertaining and researching writer, D'Israeli. They seem to be an irritable set, and I wish myself well out of it. What the devil had I to do with scribbling? It is too late to inquire, and all regret is useless. But, an' it were to do again, I should write again, I suppose. Such is human nature—at least, my share of it; though I shall think better of myself, if I have sense to stop now. If I have a wife, and that wife have a son—by anybody—I will bring up mine heir in the most unpoetic way: make him a lawyer, or a pirate—anything. But if he writes, too, I shall be sure he is none of mine, and cut him off with a Bank token. Sparred with Jackson again yesterday morning, and shall to-morrow. *Mem.* Attend the pugilistic dinner, Marquis Huntley is in the chair. Yesterday, dined *tete-a-tete* at the 'Cocoa' with Scrope Davies; sat from six till midnight; drunk between us one bottle of champagne, and six of claret, neither of which wines ever affect me. Offered to take Scrope home in my carriage, but he was tipsy and pious, and I was obliged to leave him on his knees, praying to I know not what purpose or pagod."

At the commencement of 1814, Byron again visited Newstead. On the 22nd of January he wrote to Mr. Murray: "You will be glad to hear of my safe arrival here. The time of my return will depend upon the weather, which is so impracticable, that this letter has to pass through more snows than ever opposed Napoleon's retreat. The roads are impassable, and return impossible, for the present; which I do not regret, as I am much at my ease, and six-and-twenty complete this day—a very pretty age, if it would always last. Our coals are excellent, our fireplaces large, my cellar full, and my head empty; and I have not yet recovered my joy at leaving London. If any unexpected turn occurred with my purchasers, I believe I should hardly quit the place at all, but shut my door, and let my beard grow."

The religious, or rather, perhaps, *ir*religious opinions of Byron, were about this time (the early part of 1814) very severely attacked in various ways, both in prose and verse. Writing to Mr. Murray respecting one of these writers, who had applied to that gentleman to publish his work, his lordship says: "He is wrong in one thing—I am no *Atheist:* but if he thinks I have published principles tending to such opinions, he has a perfect right to controvert them."

A few days after the note just quoted, his lordship writes to Mr. Moore, from the "Albany": "I am just returning to town, (April 9th) from which you may infer that I have been out of it; and I have been boxing, for exercise, with Jackson for this last month daily. I have also been drinking; and, and on one occasion, with three other friends at the 'Cocoa Tree,' from six till four, yea, five in the morning. We clareted and champagned till two, and then supped, and finished with regency punch, composed of Madeira, brandy, and *green* tea, no *real* water being admitted therein. There was a night for you! without once quitting the table, except to ambulate home, which I did alone, and in utter contempt of a hackney-coach, and my own *vis.* I have also, more or less, been breaking a few of the favourite commandments; but I mean to pull up and marry, if any one will have me."

The following is an account of a supper partaken of by Moore and Lord Byron, after the latter had been at a pugilistic exhibition: "As this supper," says his lordship's biographer, "may convey some idea of Lord Byron's irregular mode of diet, and thus account, in part, for the frequent derangement of his health, I shall here attempt, from recollection, a description of his supper on this occasion. We were to have been joined by Lord R——, who however did not arrive, and the party accordingly consisted but of ourselves. Having taken upon me to order the repast, and knowing that Lord Byron, for the last two days, had done nothing towards sustenance, beyond taking a few biscuits, I desired that we should have a good supply of at least two kinds of fish. My companion, however, confined himself to lobsters, and of these finished two or three, to his own share, interposing, sometimes, a small liquor-glass of strong white brandy, sometimes a tumbler of very hot water, and then neat brandy again, to the amount of nearly half-a dozen small glasses of the latter, without which, alternately with hot water, he appeared to think the lobster could not be digested. After this we had claret, of which having despatched two bottles, at about four o'clock in the morning we parted."

At the latter end of August, Lord Byron returned to Newstead again for a short while, and for the last time. On the 15th of September, he wrote to Mr. Moore: "This is the fourth letter I have began to you within the month. Whether I shall finish or not, or burn it like the rest, I know not. When we meet I shall explain *why* I have not asked you here, as I wished—with a great many other *whys* and wherefores, which will keep cold. In short, you must excuse all my seeming omissions, and commissions, and grant me more *re*mission than St. Athanasius will to yourself, if you lop off a single thread of mystery from his pious puzzle. It is my creed (and it may be St. Athanasius's, too,) that your article on T——will get somebody killed, and *that* on the *Saints* get him d—d afterwards, which will be quite enow for one number. Now for a little egotism. My affairs stand thus: to-morrow, I shall know whether a circumstance of importance, enough to change many of my plans, will occur or not. If it does not, I am off for Italy next month, and London in the mean time next week. I have got back Newstead, and twenty-five thousand pounds, (out of twenty-eight paid already) as a 'sacrifice,' the late purchaser calls it, and he may choose his own name. I have paid off some of my debts, and contracted others; but I have a few thousand pounds, which I can't spend after my own heart in this climate, and so I shall go back to the south. Hobhouse, I think, will go with me; but whether he will or not, I shall. All this, however, depends upon an event, which may, or may not, happen. Whether it will I shall probably know to-morrow; and if it does, I can't well go abroad at present."

His own account, in his memoranda, of the circumstances which led to this second offer to Miss Milbanke, his first having been rejected, appears to have been as follows: A person, who, for some time had stood high in his affections and confidence, observing how cheerless and unsettled was the state both of his mind and prospects, strenuously advised him to marry; and after much discussion, he consented. The next point for consideration was, who was to be the object of his choice; and while his friend mentioned one lady, he himself named Miss Milbanke. To this, however, his adviser strongly objected, remarking to him, that Miss Milbanke had at present no fortune, and that his embarrassed affairs would not allow him to marry without one; that she was, moreover, a learned lady, which would not at all suit him. In consequence of these representations, he agreed that his friend should write a proposal for him to the other lady named, which was accordingly done; and an answer, containing a refusal, arrived as they were one morning sitting together. "You see," said Lord Byron, "that after all Miss Milbanke is to be the person; I will write to her." He accordingly wrote on the moment, and as soon as he had finished, his friend remonstrating still strongly on his choice, took up the letter, but, on reading it over, observed, "Well, really, this is a very pretty letter; it is a pity it should not go. I never read a prettier one." "Then it shall go," said Lord Byron; and so saying, sealed and sent off, on the instant, this fiat of his destiny.

A letter to his friend Moore announces the acceptance of his suit by the lady, in the following terms:

"Newstead Abbey, Sep. 20th, 1814.

"Here's to her who long
Hath waked the poet's sigh!
The girl who gave to song
What gold could never buy.

MY DEAR MOORE—I am going to be married; that is, I am accepted, and one usually hopes the rest will follow. My mother of the Gracchi (that are to be) you think too strait-laced for me, although the paragon of only children, and invested with 'golden opinions of all sorts of men,' and full of 'most blessed conditions,' as Desdemona herself. Miss Milbanke is the lady; and I have her father's invitation to proceed there in my elect capacity, which, however, I cannot do until I have settled some business in London, and got a blue coat. She is said to be an heiress, but of that I really know nothing certainly, and shall not inquire; but I do know that she has talents, and excellent qualities; and you will not deny her judgment, *after having refused six suitors, and taken me*, Now, if you have anything to say against this, pray do; my mind is made up, positively fixed, determined, and therefore I will listen to reason, because it can do no harm. Things may occur to break it off, but I will hope not. In the meantime, I tell you (a *secret*, by-the-by—at least, till I know she wishes it to be public,) that I have proposed, and am accepted. You need not be in a hurry to wish me joy, for one may'nt be married for months. I am going to town to-morrow, but expect to be here again within a fortnight; perhaps you will meet me at Nottingham, and come over with me here. I need not say that nothing will give me greater pleasure. I must, of course, reform thoroughly; and, seriously, if I can contribute to her happiness, I shall secure my own. She is so good a person, that—that—in short, I wish I was better."

On his arrival at London, and taking up his lodgings at the "Albany," he received an invitation to a party from the Countess of ——, to which he returned the following answer:

"DEAR LADY ———. Your recollection and invitation do me great honour; but I'm going to be 'married, and can't come.' My intended is two hundred miles off, and the moment my business here is arranged, I must set off out in a great hurry to be happy. Miss Milbanke is the good-natured person who has undertaken me, and, of course, I am very much in love, and as silly as all single gentlemen must be in that sentimental situation. I have been accepted these three weeks; but when the event will take place, I do not know. One can be sure of nothing; but, at present, there appears no other interruption to this intention, which seems as mutual as possible, and now no secret. * * * You perhaps know the lady. She is niece to Lady Melbourne, and cousin to Lady Cowper, and others of your acquaintance, and has no fault, except being a great deal too good for me, and that *I* must pardon, if nobody else should. It might have been two years ago, and, if it had, would have saved me a world of trouble. She has employed the interval in refusing about half-a-dozen of my particular acquaintance, (as she did me once, by the way,) and has taken me at last, for which I am very much obliged to her. I wish it was well over, for I do hate bustle, and there is no marrying without some."

A few days afterwards, he writes to Moore: "I hope to get out of town and be married, but I shall take Newstead in my way; and you must meet me at Nottingham, and accompany me to mine Abbey. I will tell you the day when I know it. P.S. By the way, my wife elect is perfection, and I hear of nothing but her merits and her wonders, and that she is 'very pretty.' Her expectations I am told are very great; but *what*, I have not asked; nor have I seen her this *ten months*."

He writes again to Moore, on the same engrossing subject, before leaving town.

"October 14th, 1814.

"An' there were anything in marriage that would make a difference, between my friends and me, particularly in your case, I would 'none on't.' My agents sets off for Durham next week, and I shall follow him, taking Newstead and you in my way. I certainly did not address Miss Milbanke with these views, but it is likely she may prove a considerable *parti*. All her father can give, or leave her, he will, and from her childless uncle, Lord Wentworth, whose barony it is supposed will devolve on Lady Milbanke, (his sister) she has expectations. She is an only child, and Sir R.'s estates, though dipped by electioneering, are considerable. Part of them are settled on her; but whether that will be dowered now, I do not know; though, from what has been intimated to me, it probably will. The lawyers are to settle this among them, and I am getting my property into matrimonial array, and myself ready for the journey to Seaham, which I must make in a week or ten days. I certainly did not dream that she was attached to me, which it seems she has been for some time. I also thought her of a very cold disposition, in which I was also mistaken. As to her virtues, &c., &c., you will hear enough of them, (for she is a kind of pattern in the north) without my running into a display on the subject. It is well that one of us is in such fame, since there is sad defect in the *morale* of that article on my part."

"In the beginning of the month of December," says his

biographer, "being called up to town by business, I had opportunity, from being a good deal in my noble friend's society, of observing the state of his mind, and feelings under the prospect of the important change he was now about to undergo; and it was with pain I found that those sanguine hopes, with which I had sometimes looked forward to the happy influence of marriage, in waneing him over to the brighter and better side of life, were by a view of all the circumstances of his present destiny, considerably diminished; while at the same time, not a few doubts and misgivings, which had never before so strictly occurred to me, with regard to his own fitness, under any circumstances, for the matrimonial tie, filled me altogether with a degree of foreboding anxiety as to his fate, which the unfortunate event that followed but too soon fully justified."

It appears that on his lordship's arrival in town, he had, upon making a strict inquiry into the state of his affairs, found them in so utterly embarrassed a condition, as to fill him with some alarm, and even to suggest to his mind the prudence of deferring his marriage. But the die was cast—the engagement had been solemnly entered into—the day had been fixed—and he had now no alternative but to proceed. Accordingly, at the end of December, accompanied by his friend Mr. Hobhouse, he set out for Seaham, the seat of Sir Ralph Milbanke, the lady's father, in the county of Durham, and on the 2nd of January, 1815, was married.

"I saw him stand
Before the altar, with a gentle bride;
Her face was fair, but was not that which made
The starlight of his boyhood: as he stood
Even at the altar, o'er his brow there came
The self-same aspect, and the quivering shock,
That in the antique oratory shook
His bosom in his solitude; and then,
As in that hour—a moment o'er his face,
The tablet of unutterable thoughts
Was traced; and then it faded as it came,
And he stood calm and quiet, and he spoke
The fitting vows, but heard not his own words,
And all things reeled around him; he could see
Not that which was, nor that which should have been,
But the old mansion, and the accustomed hall,

And the remembered chambers, and the place,
The day, the hour, the sunshine and the shades,
All things pertaining to that place and hour,
And her who was his destiny, came back,
And thrust themselves between him and the light:
What business had they there at such a time?

This touching picture, from one of his poems, agrees, in many of its circumstances, so closely with his own prose account of the wedding, in his memoranda, that it cannot be other than interesting to introduce it here. In that memoir he describes himself as waking on the morning of his marriage, with the most melancholy reflections, on seeing his wedding-suit spread out before him. In the same mood he wandered about the grounds alone, till he was summoned for the ceremony, and joined, for the first time, on that day, the bride and her family. He knelt down, he repeated the words after the clergyman; but a mist was before his eyes,—his thoughts were elsewhere; and he was awakened by the congratulations of the bystanders, to find that he was—married.

The same morning the wedded pair left Seaham for Halnaby, another seat of Sir Ralph Milbanke, in the same county. When about to depart, Lord Byron said to his bride, "*Miss Milbanke*, are you ready?"—a mistake which the lady's confidential attendant seems to have considered as a bad omen.

In a letter to Moore, dated 2nd February, he says: "Since I wrote last I have been transferred to my father-in-law's, with my lady and my lady's maid, &c., &c., and the treacle-moon is over, and I am awake, and find myself married. My spouse and I agree, too, and in admiration. Swift says, 'no *wise* man ever married;' but for a fool, I think it is the most ambrosial of all future states. Here follows one of those breaks out of loose feeling which shows, after all, how little at ease Byron was in his new situation, and how much his heart was still among the scenes to which he had been so long accustomed. "Pray tell me what is going on in the way of intriguery, and how the w—s and rogues of the upper beggars' opera go on—or rather off—in, or after marriage; or who are going to break any particular commandment. Upon this dreary coast we have nothing but county meetings and shipwrecks; and I have dined this day upon fish, which probably dined upon the crews of several colliers, lost in the last gales. But I saw the sea once more in all the glories of surf and foam, almost equal to the Bay of Biscay. My papa, Sir Ralpho, hath recently made a speech at a Durham tax meeting; and not only at Durham, but here, several times since, after dinner. He is now, I believe, speaking to himself, (I left him in the middle) over various decanters, which can neither intercept him, nor fall asleep, as might possibly have been the case with some of his audience. PS. I must now go to tea; d—n tea. I wish it was Kinnaird's brandy, and with you to lecture me about it."

The habits of his lordship's life, and the sort of society he still frequented, towards the close of the first year of his marriage, may be judged of, from the following extract from a letter written to Mr. Moore, about the close of October:

"Yesterday, I dined out with a largeish party, where were Sheridan and Colman, Harry Harris, C.G., and his brother. Sir Gilbert Heathcoate, Dr Kinnaird, and others, of note and notoriety. Like other parties of the kind, it was first silent, then talky, then argumentative, then disputatious, then unintelligible, then altogethery, then inarticulate, and then drunk. When we had reached the last step of this glorious ladder, it was difficult to get down again without tumbling; and to crown all, Kinnaird and I had to conduct Sheridan down a cursed corkscrew staircase, which had certainly been constructed before the discovery of fermented liquors, and to which no legs, however crooked, could accommodate themselves. We, however, deposited him safe at home, where his man, evidently accustomed to the business, waited to receive him in the hall. Both he and Colman were, as usual, very good; but I carried away much wine, and the wine had previously carried away my memory; so that all was hiccup and happiness for the last hour or so, and I am not impregnated with any of the conversation. My paper is full, and I have a grevious headache. P.S. Lady B. is in full progress. Next month will bring to light (with the creed of Juno Lucina) the tenth wonder of the world—Gill Blas being the eighth—and he (my son's father) the ninth."

The following note to his friend Moore announces the completion of the event anticipated in the note just quoted: "The little girl was born on the 10th of December last; her name is Augusta Ada (the second a very antique family name —I believe not used since the time of King John). She was, and is, very flourishing and fat, and reckoned very large for her days; squalls and sucks incessantly. Are you answered? The mother is doing very well, and up again."

In some portions of this letter, not quoted, there was a kind of feeling, and a manner of expression, in reference to his present condition and future prospects, which raised the sensibilities of his friend, in reference to some apprehended coming calamity, to a very painful degree of excitement. The following is the manner in which Mr. Moore expresses himself in reference to it: "On reading over the foregoing letter, I was much struck by the tone of melancholy that pervaded it; well knowing it to be the habit of the writer's mind to seek relief, when under the pressure of any disquiet or disgust, in that sense of freedom which told him that there were homes for him elsewhere. I had, indeed, at the time, when he sent me those melancholy verses,

'There's not a joy this world can give,' &c.

felt some vague apprehension as to the mood into which his spirits then seemed to be sinking, and, in acknowledging the receipt of the verses, tried to banter him out of it. My absence from London, during the whole of this year, had deprived me of all opportunities of judging, for myself, how far the appearances of his domestic state gave promise of happiness. The strong and affectionate terms in which, soon after the marriage, he had, in some of his letters, declared his happiness—a declaration which his known frankness left me no room to question—had, in no small degree, tended to still those apprehensions, which my first view of the lot he had chosen for himself awakened. I could not, however, but observe that these indications of a contented heart soon ceased. His mention of the partner of his home became more rare and formal; and there was observable, I thought, through some of his letters, a feeling of unquiet and weariness that brought back all those gloomy anticipations with which I had, from the first, regarded his fate. I thus noticed to him the impression it had made upon me: 'And so you are a whole year married!—

It was but last year I vowed to thee
That fond impossibility.

Do you know, my dear B., there was something in your last letter—a sort of unquiet mystery, as well as a want of your usual elasticity of spirit—which has hung upon my mind unpleasantly ever since. Do tell me you are happier than that letter has led me to fear, and I shall be satisfied.' "

It was a few weeks after this communication had been made, that Lady Byron adopted the resolution of parting from her husband. She had left London about the middle of January on a visit to her father's house in Leicestershire,, and Lord Byron was in a short time to follow her. They had parted in the utmost apparent kindness; she wrote him a letter, full of playfulness and affection, on the road, and immediately on her arrival at Kirkby Mallory, her father wrote to acquaint Lord Byron that she would no more return to him. At the time when he had to stand this unexpected shock, his pecuniary embarrassments,—which had been fast gathering round him during the whole of the last year—were as bad as they well could be, (there having been no less than eight or nine executions in his house in London, in that period, besides one at Newstead, put in by Mr. Brothers, upholsterer, of Nottingham, for £1,500, the cost of furnishing the house, when his lordship first entered on the Abbey.) At this time, when, to use his own strong expressions, he was " standing alone on his hearth, with his household goods shivered around him," he was also doomed to receive the startling intelligence that the wife who had just parted with him in kindness, had parted with him—for ever.

On the 25th of April, 1816, he, for the last time, took leave of this country, and sailed for Ostend.

The circumstances under which Lord Byron now took leave of England were such as, in the case of any ordinary person, could not be considered as otherwise than extremely disastrous and humiliating. He had, in the course of one short year, gone through every variety of domestic misery; had seen his hearth eight or nine times profaned by the visitation of the coarse agents of the law, and been only saved from a prison by the privileges of his rank. He had alienated, so far as they had ever been his, the affections of his wife; and now—rejected by her, and condemned by the world—was betaking himself to an exile which had not even the dignity of appearing voluntary, as the excommunicating voice of society seemed to leave him no other resource.

After this, Newstead was again a desolation, in consequence of the sale under the *execution*, in the latter part of 1815, or in the early part of 1816; and so it remained till 1818, when it was purchased by its present esteemed owner and occupant, Colonel Wildman, for about £100,000. The gallant colonel had been school-fellow with the poet, and sat on the same form with him at Harrow.

The following is an extract from a letter written by his lordship to Colonel Wildman, immediately after the purchase, expressing not only the regard he felt for his old school-fellow, but also his evident satisfaction that the place which had cost him "more than words to part with," had fallen into hands likely to raise the venerable and romantic pile to something like its former grandeur. He says: "I should regret to trouble you with any requests of mine, in regard to the preservation of any signs of my family, which may still exist at Newstead, and leave everything of that kind to your own feelings, present or future, upon the subject. * * * I trust that Newstead will, being yours, remain so; and that it may see you as happy, as I am very sure you will make your dependants. With regard to myself, you will be sure, that whether in the fourth, or fifth, or sixth form at Harrow, or in the fluctuations of after life, I shall always remember with regard my old school-fellow—fellow-monitor and friend; and recognize with respect the gallant soldier, who, with all the advantages of fortune, and allurements of youth to a life of pleasure, devoted himself to the duties of a nobler order, and will receive his reward in the esteem and admiration of his country."

Such were the sentiments and aspirations of Lord Byron, on learning to whom the ancient home of his fathers had been disposed; and nobly and generously has the gallant owner done justice to those aspirations, and the confidence in his liberality so feelingly expressed by the poet; for not only has he expended immense sums, under guidance of the most perfect good taste, in the restoration and adornment of the Abbey, and the increase of its ornamental pleasure-grounds, but he has preserved, with a feeling of religious care, every memorial of the highly-gifted individual, formerly its possessor, which could, even in the least degree, interest those who are the admirers of his genius; and who, that has a spark of sensibility in his nature—however he may lament the errors of his life—is not so?

From the period of his departure from his native land, on his second pilgrimage, until his death, Byron employed much of his time in writing: and gave to the world, in rapid succession, that series of splendid poems, the titles of which are too well known to need here recapitulating. *Childe Harold*, however, is the work upon which, as a poet, the fame of Lord Byron, with posterity, will principally rest. Had he, indeed, written nothing else but the *fourth canto* of that glorious poem, he had done enough to secure for himself an imperishable name among the classic poets—the men of true inspiration—of his native land.

On the 15th of July, 1824, the body of the noble bard, who had died at Missolonghi, in Greece, on the 19th of April preceding, arrived at Nottingham, and was deposited in one of the rooms on the ground floor of the Blackmoor's Head Inn, High-street; where, during the course of the evening, it was visited by many hundreds of persons. On the following morning, accompanied by a procession of carriages, and a train of several thousands of pedestrians, it was removed to Hucknall Torkard Church, where it was deposited in the family vault, at that place, beside the remains of his mother.

To the kindness and liberality of Colonel Wildman, thousands, like ourselves, on this occasion, are indebted, by the privilege of traversing the spacious galleries, and venerable halls, and sacred chambers, of this noble mansion—consecrated in the mind by tender association with the glories of the past, and the triumphs of art, and genius, and valour, of more recent times—for some of the most delightful hours of their lives.

But the whistle of the train may be heard in the distance; and as we have now finished our repast, over which we have indulged in this pleasant gossip, while seated in the humble, but respectable, hostelry. at Linby, we must prepare to bid adieu to Newstead, and its classic environs.

www.ingramcontent.com/pod-product-compliance
Ingram Content Group UK Ltd.
Pitfield, Milton Keynes, MK11 3LW, UK
UKHW051704280225
4809UKWH00045B/659

9 781241 602840